D1165923

Hinduism and Christianity

Hinduism
and Christianity

Jesus Christ and His Teachings
in the light of Vedanta

by Swami Satprakashananda

(Author of *Methods of Knowledge*
and other Vedantic treatises)

VEDANTA SOCIETY OF ST. LOUIS

1975

Copyright © 1975 by the Vedanta Society of St. Louis
All rights reserved. No part of this book may be reproduced
in any form without written permission.

Standard Book Number ISBN 0-916356-53-1
Library of Congress Catalog Card Number 75-32598

Those further interested in the teachings
in this book are encouraged to visit or write:
Vedanta Society of St. Louis
205 South Skinker Boulevard
St. Louis, Missouri 63105

Contents

	Preface	7
I	What Is Hinduism?	9
II	Hinduism and Christianity	18
III	Great Teachers and Divine Incarnation	32
IV	Sri Ramakrishna and Jesus Christ	47
V	Christ, the Messenger *by* Swami Vivekananda	63
VI	The Kingdom of God is Within You	83
VII	Resist not Evil	97
VIII	The Divine Law of Karma	110
IX	Divine Grace	123
X	Ye Must be Born Again	136
XI	Worshipping God in Spirit and in Truth	148
XII	Ye Shall Know the Truth	164
XIII	Crucifixion and Death	174
XIV	Resurrection and Everlasting Life	184
	Index	191

Preface

IT IS AN historical fact that all the eight major religions of the world — Judaism, Christianity, Islam, Zoroastrianism, Hinduism (the Vedic religion), Buddhism, Confucianism, Taoism — are, without exception, of Asiatic origin.

Because of their diversities the founders of these religions are adored by their followers in different ways. Moses, Confucius, and Mohammed are regarded as prophets; Zoroaster and Lao-tse as messengers of God; while Jesus Christ and Sri Krishna are worshipped as Divine Incarnations.

Due to this close relationship between Hinduism and Christianity, there are many common features in the two religions. It is the special purpose of this book to dwell on these points as far as possible

In a general sense the founders of all the religions of the world can be regarded as saviors. They appeared at times of great distress when lawlessness and vice prevailed, and saved their peoples by establishing moral laws, religious practices, and spiritual disciplines according to the needs of the situation.

Before I conclude I must express my heavy debt of gratitude to my Vedanta students for the preparation of the manuscript, which is based primarily on the transcripts of my lectures on relevant topics.

Vedanta Society
of St. Louis
August 27, 1975

The author.

CHAPTER I

What is Hinduism?

H INDUISM is, truly speaking, the religion and philosophy of Vedanta. In all probability it is the oldest of all the religious and philosophical systems in the world.

Vedanta is established on eternal and universal principles which never become obsolete. These principles have an appeal to the human mind and are applicable to human life under all conditions. The term *Vedanta* literally means the *anta* — culmination or end — of the *Vedas*. The original Vedic texts collected and classified under four distinct headings constitute the four *Vedas,* from which the religio-philosophical system known as Hinduism is derived.[1]

[1] *Hindu* and *Hinduism* are foreign designations, as are *India* and *Indians.* The former two came from the Persians and the latter two from the Greeks. Toward the close of the sixth century B.C. the Persians under Darius I, whose empire extended from the Eastern border of Greece to the western border of India, occupied a territory closed to the river *Sindhu,* the Sanskrit name of the Indus. The Persians mispronounced *Sindhu* as

The primary name of Hinduism is *Vaidika-dharma* (the Vedic religion). It is also called *Sanatana-dharma* (the Eternal religion) because it upholds the fundamental truths which are eternal and universal. The Sanskrit term for religion is *dharma,* which includes both moral observance and spiritual living. Sometimes the word *dharma* is used only in the sense of virtue or moral observance, but usually it is closely associated with spiritual principles, particularly in Vedantic literature. One cannot develop competence for spiritual living without moral observance.

The Vedic texts are divided by subject matter into two distinct parts: the work section, and the knowledge section.

The work section of the Vedas is devoted to man's active life, to his search for temporal values, and dwells on the development of life in different stages. In the secular approach to life, one cannot get beyond the cycle of birth, death, and rebirth. Anything that is done for temporal purposes in this world comes under the work section, which is preparatory to the knowledge section.

The purpose of the knowledge section is to take man out of this temporal order and establish him in eternal life,

Hindu, and gradually the inhabitants of the regions adjoining the river *Sindhu* became known as *Hindus.* In the course of time the term was extended to the entire population of the country, and their religion came to be called *Hinduism.*

The Greeks had similar difficulty in pronouncing the Sanskrit name *Sindhu.* They called the river *Indus.* Through them the country became known as India and the people as Indians. The original name of the country is *Bharatavarsa* and that of the people *Bharatavasi.* Both are often shortly called *Bharata.*

absolute peace and blessedness; to take him away from the cycle of birth and death.

There is a unity of purpose between the two sections, for both intend to lead man from the search for the transitory to the search for the eternal. In the Vedantic view, there is no inherent contradiction, no unbridgeable gulf, between the secular life devoted to temporal values, and the spiritual life devoted to eternal truths. Being rightly directed the one leads to the other. According to Vedanta, worldly desires well regulated by ethical principles invariably lead to spiritual awakening.

As laid down in the Vedic social codes, the one universal duty of all human beings, irrespective of religious views, social rank, cultural standing, or political status, is the observance of virtue, or *dharma*. The word *dharma* means "that which upholds." It denotes particularly the "Law or Principle that upholds the world."

Dharma is that which leads to the attainment of happiness and prosperity in this world. It is through *dharma* that man can have progress in the true sense, development in the true sense, and achievement and well-being in all fields. You may enjoy the world in every way, you may seek whatever you like. The one condition Vedanta imposes is that under no circumstances should one deviate from the path of virtue.

The *Mahabharata*[1] says "Virtue protects him who protects her."

[1] *The Mahabharata* is perhaps the world's longest epic poem with over 90,000 couplets, and contains the widely read *Bhagavad Gita*.

"From virtue arises happiness."

"Virtue is the only friend that accompanies man beyond death."

"To do good to others is a meritorious act, to hurt others is a sin."

Virtue is the stable basis of every aspect of individual and collective life. A man's physical, intellectual, aesthetic, as well as spiritual well-being rests on the observance of virtue.

Moral conduct sustains man's inner nature. Unless you observe moral principles — truthfulness, sincerity, charity, modesty, etc. — you cannot maintain soundness of mind. Your judgment will not be right.

Mental health has become a great problem these days. Vedanta firmly emphasizes that the one secret of mental health is adherence to moral principles. If you want to maintain soundness of mind and live the right kind of life, you must observe morality. This is fundamental.

He who observes the moral principles gets the most out of this life. When your judgment is right, you can fully utilize your resources, both external and internal. Only through moral conduct can man gain real competence in this life.

This moral observance is needed not only for man's individual life, but also for all aspects of his collective life. In civic life, social life, national life and international life, unless there is a moral basis and goodness within human hearts, there cannot be any peace in the world. There will always be conflict and all negotiation will fail, because there will be no mutual trust. No one will trust you if you depend only on diplomacy and trickery.

Without moral observance man's economic life, his political life, his social life will all fail. Vedanta holds very strongly that moral life is necessary not only for individual peace and development, but for the peace and development of the whole world.

With a firm hold on moral principles, man's life will be as good as is possible in this world. A seeker of secular good in whatever form who keeps firm on the path of virtue, gets the utmost from his capacities and situation in life. He sees life in its true light because he gains real perception, real understanding.

This inner perception also tells him that whatever we do in this life, whatever developments we make — scientific, technological, or otherwise — we cannot get out of the world of dual experience. In this world there will always be birth and death, growth and decay, construction and destruction; that is the nature of the world.

One cannot have youth without old age, light without darkness, or good without evil. Where would evil go? Away? This phenomenal world is by nature composed of both principles, good and evil. Vedanta declares that there is no *good* in the absolute sense anywhere but in God Himself.

By moral observance you get the best out of this life. And as your mind is gradually purified through the performance of virtue, you also become disillusioned with dualities. By actually experiencing power and position, learning, fame, health and wealth, beauty, pleasure and so forth — man realizes their inherent shortcomings. He says

"Oh, so these are the ultimate results of this life. So this is all there is."

The basic condition of the world does not change. Eventually each person becomes convinced there is no assurance of security in the temporal order, no prospect of unalloyed joy in this relative universe characterized by a playground of dualities.

Human life is a drama of birth, growth, decay and death — no science can remove these. When you finally understand this basic condition of life, there is still within the depths of your heart a cry for life beyond death; light beyond darkness; joy beyond sorrow. Where else but in God can human beings find this fulfillment?

Eventually all individuals become convinced that the Supreme Being alone is eternal, all-free, all-perfect; while all else is short-lived, bound, and imperfect. Unless one is disillusioned with all of the charms and glories of secular life, one cannot accept God as the sole Goal, the sole Refuge.

You can worship God for the sake of wealth, for the sake of children, for the sake of success in life — but that is not spiritual life in the true sense. Man must realize the inherent incompetence of power and prosperity to lead him to unmixed blessing.

It is not the bitterness of adversity that makes one a genuine seeker of God. It is the emptiness of affluence perceived by a virtuous man that turns his mind Godward in the true sense. When you seek God as the one Supreme Goal, that is the real beginning of spiritual life.

Through moral observance you attain a certain measure

of purification of the mind; only then can you step into spiritual life. Otherwise your mind will always be seeking something or other in this world.

Do you know what you are seeking this very moment? Vedanta says you are seeking God. You may say "No. I want a lot of money, I want a very beautiful friend." But actually you will not be satisfied.

You may gain anything you desire, any transitory pleasure in this world, but you will never be satisfied completely. You will always say "No, it is not enough for me. I want something more."

Why? Because you are a born seeker of the Eternal. How can you be satisfied with anything less? If all the treasures of the universe were collected and put at your feet, you still would not be satisfied. Your mind is set on the Eternal from the very beginning, because you are essentially pure Spirit, ever united with God. You simply have to recognize that relationship with Him.

Gradually a person will be awakened to his real Self by following the moral course. He will be disillusioned with the world, and come to know its true nature. Then he will seek God directly.

You are seeking perfection all your life. You want to make your home perfect, to dress perfect, to have a perfect husband or wife and perfect children — you want everything to be perfect. But you don't ever find that perfection. Your inherent longing for perfection cannot be satisfied anywhere else in the world but in the one Supreme Goal.

Vedanta says there is one Supreme Being who alone is

beyond all sorrows, beyond all sufferings; who alone is ever pure, free, immortal — the very perfection of existence.

And that Supreme Being is not far away from us. He is the all-pervading Self of the universe, and dwells within us as the inmost Self of all. That is why you are always seeking more of this, more of that, until you know that nothing more in this world can satisfy you. There is one Supreme Being, the all-perfect One, who alone can satisfy you forever.

To recognize one's essential unity with the Supreme Being is the ultimate Goal of life. Rightly or wrongly, every human being is moving toward that Goal.

In many different ways every water course continuously moves toward the ocean, sometimes becoming stuck behind a stone or under a tree, but in the course of time always becoming released and reaching its goal.

Similarly human minds are moving in different directions because of differing tastes, differing capacities. But whether on paths crooked or straight, right or wrong, in whatever way all human minds are moving toward the one Supreme Goal.

That alone leads to the cessation of all sufferings and the attainment of absolute peace and blessedness. That is your sole Goal.

According to Vedanta everyone is a born seeker of God, whether he knows it or not. Man is born pure, free, immortal. But unfortunately, he does not know what he really is. Covered with a veil of ignorance, you say "I am" and think that you are this body, limited and mortal. But beyond the garb of this psychophysical being there is pure

Spirit, free and immortal. That is what you really are.

That is why there is always within you a cry for perfection, for going beyond all miseries, all sufferings. In the course of time you are bound to develop this intense longing for eternal life, for realizing God. You are meant from birth for that Supreme Goal.

As Swami Vivekananda[1] says, religion is the constitutional necessity of mankind. *Dharma* is that which ultimately leads man to his real nature and the Supreme Goal.

Vedanta recognizes the different religions of the world as pathways to that one Supreme Being, who alone is all-perfect. One and the same God is called by different names; one and the same God is worshipped in different ways.

Until you recognize your essential unity with that Supreme Being — that you are essentially pure Spirit —you will never be satisfied in this world. Though you try to satisfy yourself with this mixture of good and evil, pleasure and pain; this drama of birth, growth, decay and death is inevitable.

Vedanta says the basic truth of all religion is to hold firmly to moral life. Then regardless of what path you choose, it will inevitably lead you to spiritual life and the Supreme Goal. You cannot have real pleasure, real freedom, real life anywhere in this world until you reach that Goal.

---

[1]Swami Vivekananda, monastic disciple and chief apostle of Sri Ramakrishna, represented Hinduism at the World's Parliament of Religions in Chicago in 1893, and is generally considered to have been the interpreter of Vedanta for the modern age.

CHAPTER II

Hinduism
and Christianity

ACCORDING to many great scholars, Christianity in both its early phase and later developments was directly influenced by Hindu religious ideas, as well as indirectly through Buddhism.

The reasons for such assumptions may be summarized thus: there are distinctive elements in Christianity which cannot be traced either to its Jewish source or to its Greco-Roman contact. Among these distinctive elements are its high ethical idealism, its spirit of complete renunciation and asceticism, its devotion to the God of love and grace, and its ideal of mystical union with the Divinity. These very elements can be found in Hinduism, and there are also striking resemblances between Buddhism and Christianity.

Though Hinduism is not a missionary religion like Islam, Buddhism, or Christianity, Hindu religious ideas travelled over a great part of Europe and over all of Asia from ancient times. Over land and sea routes, India had commercial relations with nearly all of the civilized world.

Hindu religious ideas were carried in this wake by the great Brahmanic teachers and through travelers, merchants, and immigrants. These ideas prevailed over the Roman Empire, over many countries of eastern Europe, and over all of Asia for centuries before Jesus Christ.

Great philosophers like Pythagoras, Plato, Philo and Plotinus were all strongly influenced by Hindu ideas.[1] To quote A. L. Basham:

> We can only say that there was always some contact between the Hellenic world and India, mediated first by the Achaemenid Empire, then by that of Seleucids, and finally, under the Romans, by the traders of the Indian ocean.
>
> Christianity began to spread at the time when this contact was closest. We know that Indian ascetics occasionally visited the West, and that there was a colony of Indian merchants at Alexandria. The possibility of Indian influence on Neo-Platonism and early Christianity cannot be ruled out.[2]

There is also evidence that Buddhism influenced Christianity as well. For about two centuries before the birth

[1]Stutfield, H.E.M., *Mysticism and Catholicism,* pp. 31, 34. London: 1925.
The mind of Plato was heavily charged with Orphic mysticism mainly derived from Asiatic sources. India, always the home of mystical devotion, probably contributed the major share. Indian mysticism passed over into Africa and Western Europe and blossomed forth in Plotinus. . .
Rawlinson, H.G., "India in European Literature and Thought," in Garratt, G.T., edit., *Legacy of India,* p 5. Oxford: 1937.
It is more likely that Pythagoras was influenced by India than by Egypt. Almost all the theories, religious, philosophical, and mathematical, taught by Pythagoras, were known in India in the sixth century B.C. . . .
[2]Basham, A.L., *The Wonder That Was India,* p. 486. London: 1954.

of Jesus Christ, a sect known as the Essenes was quite prevalent in Palestine. John the Baptist, the forerunner of Jesus Christ from whom Christ received baptism, was an Essene.

According to most authorities, the Essenes were a Buddhist sect quite unlike anything in Judaism.[1] They practiced many austerities, were vegetarians, and observed celibacy. John the Baptist was a perfect ascetic, as was Jesus Christ — a monk, penniless, homeless, depending on nothing but God.

Though it is a controversial point, in this way it can be concluded that Christianity was influenced by Buddhism and Hinduism. There are unique elements in Christianity which many feel can be explained in no other way. W.K.C. Guthrie says of the Greeks:

> Genuine Greek religion knows no mystical striving after a blessed union with God in ecstasy after an abolition of the limits of individuality in a realm beyond the conscious life.[2]

And Dr. Kenneth Kirk, former Bishop of Oxford, states:

> The ascetic outlook of the Gospels is seen to stand out of any recognizable relation with contemporary Judaism. The passages about turning the other cheek, about taking no thought for tomorrow, about laying up no treasure on earth, about forsaking parents and possessions, about bearing the cross, are foreign to the *genius* of the race.[3]

[1]The word *Essene* is derived from the Sanskrit word *asana,* meaning seat or posture (of meditation).
[2]Guthrie, W.K.C., *Orpheus and Greek Religion,* pp. 236-7. London: 1935.
[3]Kirk, Kenneth E., *Vision of God,* p. 63. London, New York: 1947.

These are the two fundamental distinctions we find in Christianity —the ascetic note, and the ideal of mystical union. Neither can be traced to a Jewish source, or to a Greco-Roman influence.

S. Radhakrishnan says of Jesus' influences:

> Jesus, as we have seen, enlarges and transforms the Jewish conceptions in the light of His own personal experience. In this process He was helped considerably by His religious environment, which included Indian influences, as the tenets of the Essenes and the Book of Enoch show. In His teaching of the Kingdom of God, life eternal, ascetic emphasis, and even future life, He breaks away from the Jewish tradition and approximates Hindu and Buddhist thought.[1]

Leaving aside these historical points, let us see some of the actual coincidences between Hinduism, its offshoot Buddhism, and Christianity.

The idea of reincarnation — or man's succession of birth, death, and rebirth, which pervades Hinduism — was not repugnant to Jesus Christ. He Himself said with regard to John the Baptist:

> Elias truly shall first come, and restore all things.
> But I say unto you, That Elias is come already, and they knew him not . . .
>
> Then the disciples understood that he spoke unto them of John the Baptist.   (St. Matt. 17:11-13)[2]

[1]Radhakrishnan, S., *Eastern Religions and Western Thought*, p. 176. Oxford: 1940.

[2]Compare St. Matt. 11:14, St. Mark 9:12.

The idea of reincarnation was not foreign to Jesus' followers either, as is demonstrated in this passage from the Gospel of St. John (9:2):

> And his disciples asked him, saying, Master who did sin, this man, or his parents, that he was born blind?

The question "did this man commit sin?" indicates the probability the man existed in a previous life; otherwise he himself could never have committed a sin to cause his blindness at birth.

The early Christian fathers also accepted the idea of reincarnation and were very much influenced by it. In fact, the idea was so prevalent among Christian teachers that the Emperor Justinian anathemized the teachings of Origen at the Council of Constantinople in 553 A.D. Origen accepted and taught reincarnation, as did St. Jerome, St. Augustine, St. Gregory and many other early Christians.

Closely tied with the idea of reincarnation is that of *karma* — the law of cause and effect on the moral plane. St. Paul stresses this law in passages such as Galatians (6:7): "Be not deceived, God is not mocked, for whatsoever a man soweth, that shall he also reap."

It is the doctrine of *karma* allied with reincarnation that explains the inequalities of life. Otherwise there is no satisfactory explanation.

Heredity cannot explain the differences without doing violence to our sense of justice. If heredity makes the difference, the parents are responsible for the sufferings a child goes through as the result of congenital defects. Predestination also cannot explain the inequalities of life without doing injustice to our sense of God's impartiality.

Nothing else determines man's course here or elsewhere but what he accumulates within himself in past and present lives. Every thought we think, every word we speak, every deed we do is *karma* — which immediately or eventually determines situations in life for us.

Reincarnation allied with the doctrine of *karma* has been accepted by many great thinkers of the world from very ancient times, among them Plato, Voltaire, and Nietzsche.

In keeping with the doctrine of *karma,* which guarantees future reactions for all present actions, the idea of non-resistance is very prominent in Christianity. Jesus Christ taught ethical precepts such as "Resist not evil," "Love your enemies," and "Bless them that persecute you."

We find the exact parallel of these teachings in Buddhism. Six hundred years before Christ, Buddha taught:

> Let a man overcome anger by love, let him overcome evil by good; let him overcome the greedy by generosity, and a liar by the truth. For hatred does not cease by hatred at any time; hatred ceases by love, this is an old rule. (*Dhammapada,* vs. 5)

In Hinduism the teaching of non-resistance was proclaimed centuries before Buddha by Sri Krishna in the *Bhagavatam*[1] (XI: 22.57,58):

> Even though scolded by the wicked, or insulted,

[1] Sri Krishna is one of the most widely worshipped Incarnations of God in Hinduism. The *Bhagavatam* is one of the most authoritative Sanskrit scriptures, and dwells specifically on the love and knowledge of God.

ridiculed, calumniated, beaten, bound, robbed of his living, or spat upon or otherwise abominably treated by the ignorant — being thus variously shaken and placed in dire extremities, the man who desires his well-being should deliver himself by his own effort [through patience and non-resistance].

Renunciation was another important teaching of Jesus Christ: "Take no thought for tomorrow," "You cannot serve God and mammon." In the Gospel of St. Luke (18:28-30) we find:

> Then Peter said, Lo, we have left all, and followed thee. And He said unto them, Verily I say unto you, There is no man that hath left house, or parents or brethren, or wife, or children, for the kingdom of God's sake,
>
> Who shall not receive manifold more in this present time, and in the world to come, life everlasting.

This idea of renunciation has been taught in India from very ancient times. In the *Upanishads* we find: "Immortality can be attained not through progeny, not through wealth. Only a few can reach it through renunciation, abandoning everything for the sake of the Lord, to whom everything belongs."

From time immemorial there have been millions of persons who dedicated their lives completely to the search for God, giving up everything — penniless, homeless, carrying on the tradition that Buddha and Jesus represented. People of high rank and position turned their backs upon all future prospects in their search for the

Eternal, their search for the Highest. That tradition is practiced in India even today. In both Hinduism and Buddhism we find this ideal of asceticism and renunciation prevalent.

In Hinduism and Christianity however, we find another element which we do not find emphasized in Buddhism, and that is the idea of the grace of God. Sri Krishna very much stressed this idea in the *Bhagavad Gita*[1] (X:8):

> I am the origin of everything, everything arises out of Me; by knowing this men offer everything to Me and worship Me with loving devotion.

Further (VII:14):

> It is very difficult to cross this ocean of mortality, this phenomenal world, to reach the Ultimate, the Real, where there is absolute peace and blessedness. But those who take refuge in Me alone cross this ocean.

In this way a life of complete self-surrender, devotion to God, and dependence upon His grace has been emphasized in the *Bhagavad Gita* and many other Hindu texts.

In later Hindu literature we find aphorisms on devotion and grace:

"What is bhakti, what is devotion?" "It is supreme love for God."

"What is the character of God?" "He from whom proceeds the origin, the preservation and dissolution of the universe — omnipotent, all-powerful, omnipresent."

---

[1]Literally the "Song of God," the *Bhagavad Gita* is the Gospel of Hinduism, and gives practical instruction in spiritual disciplines.

But at the same time God is all-love, inexpressible; a Hindu devotee is especially concerned with loving God. He is not particularly concerned with God's majesty and glory, splendor or power. The devotee wants the grace of the benign, all-gracious Lord who alone can rescue him from all bondages.

The concept of grace in Christianity is demonstrated in many passages in the New Testament. Jesus Christ says:

> I am the bread of life: he that cometh to me shall never hunger, and he that believeth on me shall never thirst.
> > (St. John 6:35)
> But seek ye first the kingdom of God and his righteousness; and all these things shall be added unto you.
> > (St. Matt. 6:33)

And in Ephesians (2:5) St. Paul writes: "By grace you are saved." Jesus' parable of the prodigal son in St. Luke (15:11-32) is also a beautiful illustration of the boundless grace of God.

There are many other passages in the Bible which can be explained from the Hindu viewpoint. Jesus Christ emphasizes purity of heart: "Blessed are the pure in heart for they shall see God." Hindu scriptures say "By mind you are to see That," that is, by the purified mind.

The mind is not clear enough, not tranquil and transparent enough for the perception of truth. The moment the mind is purified, truth is there. "Know the truth and the truth will make you free." (St. John 8:32)

Why? Hindu teachers say because the truth is that you are ever in God. You do not have to seek Him. He is omnipresent — open your inner eye and see Him. Jesus said:

> The light of the body is the eye: if therefore thine eye be single, thy whole body shall be full of light. (St. Matt. 6:22)

All search for God simply means the purification of the mind. There is truly no search; God is hidden by your ignorance. Through purification your mental eye is opened, you see God, and you become free from all bondages. That is the greatest beatitude.

"The Kingdom of God is within you." (St. Luke 17:21) This passage can be explained by the Hindu doctrine that the self of man is ever united with the Supreme Self — birthless, decayless, deathless — you are really pure, free, illumined. When you become aware of this truth, you are free.

Jesus said "Be ye perfect, even as the Father which is in Heaven is perfect." The Hindu takes this literally. You are already perfect, your impurities have only to be removed for you to discover your essential unity with God.

The reason for this unity is God's creation of the world; everything in existence proceeded from Him. We read in the fourth Gospel:

> In the beginning was the Word, and the Word was with God, and the Word was God; the same was in the beginning with God.
>
> All things were made by him; and without him was not anything made that was made.
>
> In him was life; and the life was the light of men.
>
> And the word was made flesh, and dwelt among us, (and we beheld his glory, the glory as of the only begotten of the Father), full of grace and truth.   (St. John 1:1-4,14)

A very similar passage can be found in the *Brahmanas,* possibly the oldest religious literature in the world: "In the beginning the Lord of the Universe alone existed. With him *Vak* [word or speech] was the second, and *Vak* is verily the Supreme *Brahman.*"[1] Shankara, the great Hindu teacher who lived much later (7th century A.D.), also declares that the Word precedes creation.

According to many authorities, St. John received this idea of the Word from Philo, a Jewish mystic well-versed in Greek and Oriental thought who lived in Alexandria, the great meeting place of Eastern and Western cultures. Philo was quite likely influenced by Indian thought, and in turn influenced early Christianity. Charles Bigg states:

> It is probable that Philoism colored the New Testament itself, and it is certain that it largely affected the after-development of Christian doctrine.[2]

Philo recognized the Word as "the only begotten son of God" (directly produced by God). Similarly in the Hindu view *Vak* can be conceived as "the only begotten son of God," but becoming manifest in human form in different ages and in different climes.

This is the difference between the Christian and Hindu views on this subject. According to Christian theology, the Word has been manifest once and for all in human form as the historical Jesus Christ. But according to the Hindu view

[1] *Brahman,* the all-pervading Supreme Reality of Vedanta philosophy, is essentially pure Being-Consciousness-Bliss. <u>That</u> alone exists in the absolute sense.

[2] Bigg, Charles, *Christian Platonists of Alexandria,* p. 49. Oxford: 1913.

the Incarnation of God is an eternal truth, and *Vak* is not identified with one particular historical form.

There are two lines of creation from the Word. One is the general creation or "mass production" of all animate and inanimate things and beings, indicated clearly by St. John: "All things were made by him."

The other is the special creation or special handicraft of God, Jesus Christ, and in the Hindu view other Incarnations as well. Hindus believe that Jesus Christ is but one of the manifestations of the Word, but Christianity has identified that Word solely with Jesus Christ, and accepts only one Incarnation.

Though there is this difference between the Christian and Hindu views of Divine Incarnation, devotion to God in some aspect is essential to both religions.

Sri Krishna again and again speaks of devotion, and this idea has been very well expressed in the *Bhagavatam* in "The Last Message of Sri Krishna," delivered to his devoted friend and disciple Uddhava.

> I, the dear Self of the pious, am obtainable by devotion alone, which is the outcome of faith; the devotion to Me purges even the low-born of their congenital impurities.

> Piety joined to truthfulness and compassion, or learning coupled with austerity, never wholly purifies a mind which is devoid of devotion to Me.

> As gold smelted by fire gives up its dross and gets back its real state, so the mind by means of systematic devotion to Me winnows off subtle impressions of past karma and attains to Me.

O Uddhava, neither yoga [concentration of mind], nor knowledge nor piety nor study, nor austerity, nor renunciation captivates Me so much as heightened devotion to Me.
(XI:14.21,22,33,20)

How highly Sri Krishna has spoken of devotion!

The Christian emphasis on devotion is well known. In the New Testament we find:

Keep yourselves in the love of God, looking for the mercy of our Lord Jesus Christ unto eternal life. (Jude 21)

He that loveth father or mother more than me is not worthy of me: and he that loveth son or daughter more than me is not worthy of me. (St. Matt. 10:37)

Jesus said unto him, Thou shalt love the Lord thy God with all thy heart, and with all thy soul, and with all thy mind. This is the first and great commandment. (St. Matt. 22:37,38)

The culmination of the religion of devotion in both Hinduism and Christianity is faith in the Incarnation of God. Great teachers are generally worshipped as prophets or messengers of God, or just as inspired human beings. But Hinduism and Christianity declare that God incarnates Himself in human form.

He is defined as omnipotent and omniscient — the omnipresent Ruler of the universe. He is at the same time full of boundless grace, beauty, and blessedness. That God of grace is worshipped by His devotees to get beyond the ocean of mortality.

Hindus and Christians believe that the benign Lord incarnates Himself to guide and lead erring humanity beyond the maze of worldly life to eternal life, absolute peace and blessedness.

When human beings know through devotion that God really feels for their sufferings, they can believe that He condescends to come to this earth and live like an ordinary mortal. This belief in God's Incarnation — the very culmination of the devotional approach — is found particularly in Hinduism and Christianity.

CHAPTER III

Great Teachers
and Divine Incarnation

IVINE Incarnation means the coming down of God from the transcendental plane to this physical plane, where He lives with human beings in a human form. The Sanskrit word for an Incarnation of God is *avatar,* which literally means descent. God descends to the earthly plane to set aright human affairs which have become chaotic through lack of morality and love.

Divine Incarnations come at a critical time for a race or nation. They fulfill a divine mission when righteousness subsides and irreligion prevails — when the minds of people get confused and don't know where to turn. When human beings need divine guidance, these great teachers come.

Belief in the Incarnation of God has been prevalent particularly among the Christians and Hindus, while the founders of other religions are not generally regarded by their followers as Incarnations of Divinity.

Among the greatest spiritual leaders of the world, Sri Krishna, Buddha, and Jesus Christ are worshipped by many as Incarnations of God. Moses, Confucius, and Mohammed are often thought of as prophets; while Zoroaster and Lao-tse are usually considered messengers of God.

Regardless of title, the founders of all major religions are looked upon by their followers as the highest manifestation of divine love, divine power, divine purity, and divine wisdom. Whatever power, knowledge, or grace they exhibit in their lives comes directly from God: His saving grace descends upon humanity through them.

According to Christian theology, the Incarnation of God proceeds from the second person of the Trinity — the Word. It is from this Word that the whole of creation comes, including special manifestation as the Son of God, Jesus Christ. As we find in the Gospel of St. John (1:14):

> And the Word was made flesh, and dwelt among us, (and we beheld his glory, the glory as of the only begotten of the Father), full of grace and truth.

Hinduism and Christianity both agree that it is the Word from which everything in the universe has arisen. Divine Incarnation is also an embodiment of that Word, but in human form.

Philosophers have always found great difficulty in relating the world's opposites of birth and death, good and evil, light and darkness, to the Supreme Being who is ever-free, ever-perfect. So this Word is their intermediate between that Supreme Being — the One without a second — and this manifold universe.

Word means expression, as every word is an expression of some inner idea. Words are simply the concrete forms of ideas. So *the* Word is conceived by some as the cosmic ideation, or God's first thought of this concrete universe.

Just as an architect forms an idea before giving expression to a great building, so God, the divine architect, had prior thought of this universe. And because it was His thought, it actually expressed itself as the universe.

In this sense of God's first idea or thought of creation, the Word is His first begotten, and not just Jesus Christ, but everything else has proceeded from that Word. All Incarnations, all human beings, and all material objects have proceeded from that one cosmic ideation.

This universe is the general manifestation of the Word, but there is also another, a special manifestation. This second manifestation is the Incarnation of God, or the Word incarnate in human form. "And the word was made flesh, and dwelt among us." Out of compassion for the suffering of human beings, God takes a human body and lives upon the earth.

Up to this point there is no disagreement between Hinduism and Christianity, but here the two religions differ. Christian theology has indissolubly linked the Word with a particular historical form, manifest two thousand years ago as Jesus Christ. In Christian belief He is the one Incarnation, the only begotten Son of God.

But Hindus believe Jesus Christ is not the only Incarnation of the Word in human form; they believe that Incarnation is not just an historical event which took place only once and will never happen again.

Hinduism declares the Incarnation of God to be an

eternal truth, with that one Word incarnating itself many, many times over the whole course of existence according to the needs of humanity. In the Hindu view this Word finds expression not just in the form of Jesus Christ but in Sri Krishna, Buddha, and many others in the past as well as those yet to come.

Human beings have lived on this earth for hundreds of thousands of years. Throughout man's existence God has taken care of him, wishing to provide liberation from the bondages of life. Sri Krishna says to Arjuna in the *Bhagavad Gita* (IV:5,7,8):

> Many lives have I passed through, as also yourself. Many times I have been born, but I know all this. You do not know because you are an ordinary mortal under the spell of ignorance. I am a divine person, I know how many times I have been born.

> Whenever, O Arjuna, righteousness declines, and unrighteousness prevails, I body myself forth, assume human form, and live as a human being.

> In order to protect the righteous and also to punish the wicked, I incarnate Myself on this earth from time to time.

According to the Christian point of view there is only one Incarnation of God. Hinduism says that there have been many Incarnations from time immemorial, and there will continue to be Incarnations as long as human beings live in this world and need the help of God.

Though both Hinduism and Christianity declare the Incarnation of God to be a fact, it is very difficult to convince anyone of this through reason. All of the great spiritual leaders of the world have been disregarded by many, and by their own contemporaries in particular. Sri Krishna states (B.G. IX:11):

> Unaware of My higher state as the great Lord of beings, the foolish disregard Me, dwelling in the human form.

Often God, of His own accord, accepts very humble situations on earth in which He is subject to many kinds of persecution and privation. Jesus Christ was born in a stable meant for animals, while Sri Krishna was born in a prison.

To all appearances, an Incarnation is an ordinary human being. He moves, talks, eats, and sleeps like any other mortal on earth. It is for these very reasons most persons will not accept an Incarnation of God. They say "What is he? He is just a human being like I am."

Yet though God is apparently limited when in human form, it creates no limitations for Him. This physical system does not limit Spirit. Though appearing to be a bound human being the Incarnation of God is beyond all bondages, ever possessing divine power, divine wisdom, and ever established in Spirit Consciousness. This is a most difficult thing for most persons to understand, and their acceptance is unlikely to come through speculative reasoning.

The real proof of the fact of Incarnation is to be found in the statements of the great teachers themselves. There is no reason why a person like Jesus Christ should falsely say:

> If God were your Father, ye would love me: for I proceeded forth and came from God; neither came I of myself but he sent me.   (St. John 8:42)

Similarly Sri Krishna says (B.G. IV:6):

> Though I am birthless, of changeless nature and Lord of beings, I am born in human form through My own inscrutable power.

And in the nineteenth century Sri Ramakrishna[1] said: "He who was incarnate as Rama, as Krishna, is now present here in the form of Ramakrishna." He said that the same Divine Being plunges from the Formless and appears in one place as Rama or Krishna, returns to the Formless, and again appears in another place in the form of Jesus Christ.

Through His divine will God descends to earth for the good of humanity. The real evidence for belief in such Divine Incarnation is in the words of these great teachers themselves. Of unimpeachable integrity, it is they who declare that they have come from God.

Although the revered spiritual leaders of the world may not be recognized as Incarnations of God by the different religions, they are in a class by themselves. They are different from those persons who have risen to a very high state of purity and perfection, for they do not rise from below, but descend from above. Far above the level of saints and sages, they belong to God's inner circle.

These great spiritual teachers come with a divine mission to fulfill, and they are conscious of that. With special authority they establish a new religious order which comes with a brilliance of spiritual light. Having no concern

---

[1]Sri Ramakrishna (1836-1886) is worshipped by many as an Incarnation of God. His life is compared with that of Jesus Christ in Chapter IV.

for their own welfare, their activities are all directed to the good of humanity.

Such teachers are different from ordinary spiritual leaders who work among small numbers of people for the time being, and whose power subsides and influence dwindles after they leave. The great teachers inaugurate a new order of things, and as the years pass their influence increases. This is the one big difference.

Sri Ramakrishna said ordinary teachers are like small ferry boats; somehow or other they manage to take a few passengers from shore to shore. They help just a few out of this death-bound world.

But the great spiritual leaders are like huge steamers, which can carry any number of persons for centuries to come across the ocean of mortality that is this world. Through God's grace they are able to save many, many human souls.

According to Hinduism it is unimportant whether a spiritual teacher is considered a prophet, a messenger, or worshipped as the Incarnation of God. Whatever one's view may be with regard to these spiritual leaders, the vital point is that they all have to be considered the saviors of souls.

All those in this class who start a tidal wave of spirituality in the world — whose power continues to grow with the passing of years — can be called saviors.

Whatever teachings they have presented to the world, if the spiritual aspirant follows those teachings he is sure to reach the Goal. If you follow the real teachings of Mohammed, your soul will be saved. If you sincerely follow the teachings of Moses, you will be saved. If you faithfully follow the teachings of any other great spiritual leader of the world you will certainly be saved, for all those in this class are the saviors of mankind. Their teachings are all pathways leading to the same ultimate Goal.

They form a bridge, as it were, between this world and the Kingdom of God. Take the bridge that suits you and you will reach the Supreme end of life. Human beings for ages after saviors pass away reach the shore of divine freedom, divine purity, divine joy along these bridges.

Another distinguishing characteristic in the lives of these great ones is their timeliness. According to the Hindu view they usually come at a critical age in the history of a nation, race, or country. There is often political or social chaos because of spiritual and moral degeneration.

At a time when superstition and callousness prevailed among the Jews, Moses came. The Buddha came when great reform in Hinduism was particularly needed. And Sri Krishna and Jesus Christ also came at especially critical times in the lives of their peoples.

When this human life requires readjustment on a large scale the Divine Being incarnates Himself in human form — to teach human beings, and to guide the benighted world towards true light.

There are, of course, differences in the manifestation of divine love, divine power, and divine wisdom in these great spiritual personalities. Still, there is a descent of divinity on earth through all of them. The differences are due mostly to the needs of the age and the psychological conditions of the people who hear the message.

In spite of apparent differences, there is one fundamental keynote which runs through all their messages: these saviors point to the true meaning of life. They turn the thoughts of people from the temporal to the eternal. This doesn't mean that they don't want people to be interested in secular affairs. They do, but they ask men and women to utilize secular values for the sake of eternal values. These secular values, however necessary they may be for earthly existence, cannot insure happiness, strength, wisdom, or freedom.

Saviors point out an approach to absolute values. They show how human beings can free themselves from the bondage of relative existence and attain the one abiding peace that is never broken, the one supreme light that never flickers or fails. This is a common element in all of their messages.

These great teachers do not want human beings to live in poverty or misery. They know that if people's moral and spiritual lives are taken care of, their material life will automatically take care of itself. Jesus Christ said to seek first the Kingdom of God and His righteousness, and all these things shall be added unto you.

But we forget these basic truths of life and cling wholeheartedly to the material aspect. This defeats its own purpose, because material life is not secure without a moral basis, and moral life is not secure without a spiritual basis. So these great spiritual leaders turn our attention to the fundamentals of life, the eternal truths on which all aspects of life must rest.

These great teachers or saviors at the same time demonstrate the highest spiritual ideals. They are the greatest exemplars of their own teachings. If you want to see the supreme demonstration of love for human beings, love for God; or the highest example of spiritual wisdom, self-sacrifice, truthfulness, or moral virtue; you must see it in their lives.

They are the greatest manifestations of God's love, God's wisdom, freedom and joy. They demonstrate what they teach, for the person is greater than the message.

Jesus Christ taught "Resist not evil. Bless them that persecute you." His life and crucifixion are the very perfection of this teaching.

Sri Krishna emphasized the virtue of non-attachment — doing your duties in life while your heart remains fixed on the Highest. While driving a war chariot in battle, he taught Arjuna the highest spiritual truths, which are recorded in the *Bhagavad Gita.*

These saviors come to set examples for humanity, by following which human beings can gain complete freedom and realize God. Jesus Christ said "I am the way, the truth, and the life: no man cometh unto the Father, but by me." By living example even more than precept, saviors teach human beings what they should do.

These great teachers come with such power that they can transform the lives of sinners into saints and sages. Imagine, Jesus Christ transformed fishermen into apostles! It takes years of hard struggle to get beyond the weaknesses that beset human beings.

Perhaps just by a thought, a touch, or a glance — great saviors can completely transform human hearts. There can be no greater miracle than this! Feeding thousands with a few fishes is not as great as making apostles out of fishermen or converting sinners into saints.

Esoteric and supernatural powers are not even as great as those of science and medicine, through which man can gain a better heart or travel into space. These other miracles are nothing, because they do not solve life's problems.

Man's primary problem is psychological, not biological, and until that problem is solved, no science, knowledge, or power can solve the other problems of life. The secret of real freedom, real wisdom, real joy, is in man's inner life.

It is by their power of transforming one's inner life that the great saviors have to be tested. Through their power of infusing a new religious spirit into the dry bones of the old we can know that they come from God.

Actually the outer forms of religion do not ever decline very much, though cultural development may suffer. People have a tendency to cling to religious books, rites, and ceremonies. But when the inner spirit of religion declines, moral life declines, and material life cannot hold its own either.

There is plenty of outward religion today; at every step you find some religious society or organization functioning. Still people do not find any real peace, real freedom, real joy. Why? Because the inner spirit is lacking — there is no real spirituality.

Great spiritual leaders come to infuse new life into the inner spirit of religion at the time it is needed most. After these great ones pass away, we find a renaissance of cultural development. There was such development in the wake of Jesus Christ, Buddha, and Mohammed. Because they work at the root of life, man's architecture, art, music, literature, and politics all develop as a result of the spiritual tidal wave set in motion by the great saviors.

If you water the root of a tree, the whole tree is taken care of. But if you forget the root and care only for the branches, you cannot keep the tree alive. Similarly the spiritual principle in man is the root of his life. Whether you wish economic, political, social, or cultural development, the inner spirit has to be cared for. Life's fulfillment is in none of these outward forms, but in inner spiritual development.

When humanity forgets that ideal of life, life as a whole will languish. It is then that the Lord manifests Himself in human form to guide the world back to spiritual principles. This is the mission of the Divine Incarnations.

Belief in the divine mission of an Incarnation of God can be found only in Hinduism and Christianity: it is the very culmination of these religions of devotion. God's Incarnation establishes the clearest relationship between human beings as they are and the Divine Being. There can be no greater proof of God's grace and love than this.

Unquestionably God gives us food to eat, air to breath, and water to drink. It is true He has endowed the face of nature with much beauty and filled many human hearts with virtues and unselfish love. But if we turn our eyes to the dark side of nature, we find it is as chaotic as it is ordered, as ferocious as it is benign. Wherever we look, we cannot find any conclusive evidence of God's kindness and grace.

Yet if it is a fact that God incarnates Himself to live among human beings more humbly than they do; that His sole purpose is to deliver us from the bondages of life, to make us free from all sins and give us absolute freedom, joy, light, and life; that for all this the Divine Being assumes human form, undergoing all manner of humiliation and persecution, then what greater proof of divine grace and love could there be? Otherwise how can we believe that God has concern for human beings?

We would have to think that God is far away and apart from us, just a mere onlooker operating somewhere else in the universe. If God is indifferent and operates regardless of suffering or enjoyment, we can't possibly love Him. You can pay homage to such a Supreme Ruler from a distance, but He cannot be a source of attraction for your soul.

We can love God only when we know of His compassion; when we know that He really feels for us. There is one test of God's mercy and only one: that He sends His own to this world to rescue humanity.

In this way when you become convinced of God's love for you, you cannot help but love God. When human beings actually recognize His divine personality in human form and feel His grace and love, their hearts are filled with whole-souled devotion to Him. It is this devotion to an Incarnation of God that is the fulfillment of both Hinduism and Christianity.

Because the Incarnations demonstrate God's love, His purity, His knowledge, His freedom, His joy — we can worship God through them. We cannot conceive of God in a better way than through His Incarnations.

> No man can really see God except through these human manifestations. If we try to see God otherwise, we make for ourselves a hideous caricature of Him and believe the caricature to be no worse than the original. There is a story of an ignorant man who was asked to make an image of the God Shiva, and who, after days of hard struggle, manufactured only the image of a monkey.
> So whenever we try to think of God as He is in His absolute perfection, we invariably meet with the most miserable failure; because as long as we are men, we cannot conceive Him as anything higher than man. The time will come when we shall transcend our human nature and know Him as He is; but as long as we are men we must worship Him in man and as man.[1]

The lives of the great spiritual leaders are the living proof of God's love. They come from above with the radiance of the Spirit to demonstrate God's love for human beings, and receive man's love for God in return.

There are two mighty and perpetual streams of love in this world. On the one hand the Supreme Lord is seeking human beings, and on the other human hearts are seeking Him. All other loves can be summed up in one or the other of these two streams.

[1]Vivekananda, S., *The Yogas and Other Works,* p. 420. New York: 1953.

The great spiritual leaders, whether you call them Incarnations, or prophets, or messengers, are the confluence of these two mighty streams. Like the small creek joining a river in order to reach the ocean, if you take refuge in the great Incarnations of God you will surely attain the divine ocean of God's love, God's freedom, God's joy.

So there is great significance in this view of Divine Incarnation. These great spiritual leaders are all saviors, because they lead the souls of human beings to eternal life, to immortal bliss.

Though there are individual differences in these manifestations of God's power and God's grace, whenever He descends in human form His love takes human beings beyond this world of mortality.

God's grace and love have become manifest many times in the past, as they will be manifest many times in the future. Out of His infinite compassion, from time to time God sends these saviors to the world to save human beings from bondages and sufferings. Through the divine authority of their exemplary lives and teachings, they have the ability to completely transform human lives.

Their sole mission is to lead human beings from the unreal to the Real, from darkness to light, from death to immortality. When we understand the divine mission of Buddha, Jesus Christ, Sri Krishna, or any of the others — and try to build our lives according to the ideals they have set for us, we receive the grace of God and attain to Him and complete freedom.

CHAPTER IV

Sri Ramakrishna and Jesus Christ

T HOUGH often separated by many centuries, we find in the lives of the world's great religious teachers certain basic similarities.

Sri Ramakrishna was born in the year 1836, more than eighteen hundred years after Jesus Christ. Yet there is no fundamental difference in their lives and teachings. The same dominant spiritual note persists in the words and actions of both.

Being born under different social and political conditions, and teaching to different audiences, there are differences in their expressions and emphasis. But though their presentations differ, the ideals Jesus Christ and Sri Ramakrishna hold before humanity are essentially the same.

Surprising incidents have been recorded with regard to the birth of both of these great spiritual leaders. These incidents seem to be miraculous, yet they are difficult to disbelieve for they come from authentic sources.

Jesus Christ and Sri Ramakrishna were both born under very humble, though unusual, circumstances. Before Mary was pregnant with Jesus Christ, an angel appeared to her:

> And the angel said unto her, Fear not, Mary: for thou hast found favour with God.

> And, behold, thou shalt conceive in thy womb, and bring forth a son, and shalt call his name Jesus.

> Then said Mary unto the angel, How shall this be, seeing I know not a man?

> And the angel answered and said unto her, The Holy Ghost shall come upon thee, and the power of the Highest shall overshadow thee: therefore also that holy thing which shall be born of thee shall be called the Son of God.

> (St. Luke 1:30- 31,34-35)

Joseph was naturally much confused by his wife's pregnancy:

> But while he thought on these things, behold, the angel of the Lord appeared unto him in a dream, saying, Joseph, thou son of David, fear not to take unto thee Mary thy wife; for that which is conceived in her is of the Holy Ghost.

> And she shall bring forth a son, and thou shalt call his name Jesus: for he shall save his people from their sins.

> (St. Matt. 1:20-21)

Other miraculous events of Jesus Christ's birth in a manger are recorded in the Gospels of St. Luke (2:1-20) and St. Matthew (2:1-13).

Sri Ramakrishna was born of very poor parents in a small hut used for husking rice. The spiritual experiences that his mother and father had before his birth have been recorded in *Sri Ramakrishna The Great Master.* Here Sri Ramakrishna's mother, Chandra, is telling her husband, Kshudiram, of a strange experience she had while he was away:

> . . . when I was speaking with [my friend] Dhani in front of the temple of the Jugis, I suddenly saw a divine light come from the holy image of the great God Shiva, fill the temple and rush towards me in waves. Taken by surprise, I was on the point of telling Dhani about it when all of a sudden the light engulfed me and swiftly entered my body.

> Stunned by wonder and fear, I fell down unconscious. Afterwards, when Dhani had helped me to recover, I told her everything. At first she was much surprised, then she said 'You had an epileptic fit.' But I have the feeling that the light has been in my womb ever since, and that I am pregnant.

Kshudiram reassures his wife, and is able to confirm her suspicions:

> Be free from all anxiety and know for certain that, whatever Raghuvir [the family diety] shows by His grace, is for our good. During my stay at Gaya, Sri Gadadhar [the God Vishnu] revealed to me, in a supernatural way, that a son would again be born to us.[1]

By supernatural means the parents of both Jesus Christ and Sri Ramakrishna knew that a son was to be born unto them, and that this son was of divine origin. Sri Ramakrishna and Jesus Christ, though without wealth,

---

[1]Saradananda, S., *Sri Ramakrishna The Great Master,* p. 36. Mylapore - Madras: 1952.

property, or any kind of earthly possessions, both proved to be uncrowned kings —the founders of spiritual empires.

Neither Jesus Christ or Sri Ramakrishna had any kind of formal education that we know of, yet they rose to be teachers of humanity. Because they had inner illumination, the whole face of Truth was revealed to them.

Sri Ramakrishna practiced hard spiritual disciplines for twelve long years of his life. We do not find any record of the practice of spiritual discipline in the life of Jesus Christ, though a long period from His twelfth to thirtieth years is not known to us. There have been persons who thought that Jesus Christ visited India during this time, but we do not have any evidence of that, or any history of His life as a spiritual aspirant. We see Him from the beginning as a full-fledged teacher.

It does seem that He must have lived a very secluded life at one time, lost completely in meditation and the search for God. Even if the great spiritual teachers do not appear to us as spiritual aspirants, they probably practiced spiritual disciplines, and it is quite likely they realized God through a particular course.

In the first three Gospels, however, we find these recorded accounts of the transfiguration of Jesus Christ. St. Matthew writes (17:1-2):

> And after six days Jesus taketh Peter, James, and John his brother, and bringeth them up into an high mountain apart.
> And was transfigured before them: and his face did shine as the sun, and his raiment was white as the light.

Similarly in St. Mark (9:2-3):

> And after six days Jesus taketh with him Peter, and James, and John, and leadeth them up into an high mountain apart by themselves: and he was transfigured before them.

> And his raiment became shining, exceeding white as snow; so as no fuller on earth can white them.

And in St. Luke (9:28-29):

> And it came to pass about an eight days after these sayings, he took Peter and John and James, and went up into a mountain to pray.

> And as he prayed, the fashion of his countenance was altered, and his raiment was white and glistering.

According to the Hindu view, this transfiguration was the state of *samadhi* — the direct inner perception of one's unity with the Divinity, realized through deep meditation and prayer. In this state of ecstatic experience all contact with the outer world is lost, and the physical body often undergoes an amazing transformation.

For a good portion of his life, Sri Ramakrishna had the experience of *samadhi* almost daily, and for this reason there are many eye-witness accounts available. The following description was written by a journalist, who observed Sri Ramakrishna in *samadhi* in 1881 while accompanying a small party aboard a river steamer:

> Except the rigidity of the body there was no quivering of the muscles or nerves, no abrupt or convulsive movement of any kind. The fingers of the two hands as they lay in his lap were slightly curled.

But a most wonderful change had come over the face. The
lips were slightly parted as if in a smile, with the gleam of the
white teeth in between. The eyes were half closed with the
balls and pupils partly visible, and over the whole
countenance was an ineffable expression of the holiest and
most ecstatic beautitude.[1]

And a disciple recorded this account of Sri
Ramakrishna at a large religious festival in 1885:

We never imagined before that such change could come
on a man's body in the twinkling of an eye under the influence
of spiritual emotions. His tall figure, as seen by us daily,
looked much taller and appeared to be as light as a body seen
in a dream.

*Getting brighter, the light dark colour of his body became
converted into a fair complexion. Brightened by the divine
mood and lit up by an incomparable smile coming out of his
slightly parted lips, his face beaming with glory, peace, bliss
and compassion, spread a wonderful light, which illumined
all sides.*

Bewitched, as it were, by the sight, the vast congregation
forgot all other things and followed him almost unknowingly. The bright ochre colour of the silk he put on, became one
with the lustre of his body and he was mistaken for a person
surrounded by flames of fire.[2] [Italics added]

As Incarnations of God, both Sri Ramakrishna and
Jesus Christ had constant vision of God everywhere,
underlying all forms of existence. Through *samadhi*, they
also realized the identity, as well as the unity, of the

[1]Gupta, Nagendranath, *Ramakrishna-Vivekananda*, quoted in Satprakashananda, S., *Methods of Knowledge*, p. 287. London: 1965.
[2]Saradananda, S. *Sri Ramakrishna The Great Master*, p. 825. Mylapore-
Madras: 1952.

individual self with the Supreme Self.

In the life of Sri Ramakrishna we have a full record of his search for this Truth. We find that he approached divinity in many different ways.

According to the Hindu view every religion is a pathway to the Supreme Being. Sri Ramakrishna was not satisfied in realizing God in one particular aspect. At first he tried to realize the Divine Mother through meditation and prayer, and he succeeded. Even then his spiritual appetite was not satisfied. He wanted to see God in all forms and aspects. So he continued his spiritual practices.

In Hinduism there are many different spiritual disciplines leading to various forms of God-realization. Sri Ramakrishna practiced all of them, meditating on God as the Divine Mother, Father, Master, Friend, Child, and Beloved. He also approached God as the impersonal absolute Being. After practicing many different courses in Hinduism, he turned to Islam, and successfully realized God as Allah. Then he turned to Christianity.

Whenever he adopted any particular spiritual course, Sri Ramakrishna put his heart and soul into that course and followed it very strictly. He would not even go into the shrine of the Kali temple where he lived. When he turned to Christianity he became suffused with the spirit of Jesus Christ, and all the Hindu gods and goddesses seemed to be pushed from his heart.

One day while in this state, with his mind filled with the thought of Jesus Christ, he viewed an oil painting of the Virgin Mary with the baby Jesus in her arms. The picture seemed to be luminous, and he felt a radiance coming from the picture and enfolding him. For three days this absorption in Jesus Christ continued.

Near the end of the third day, while Sri Ramakrishna was meditating on Christ in a grove of sacred trees, he had a vision. He saw a luminous figure proceeding slowly towards him, and at first did not know who the figure could be. He knew that it had to be a foreigner, for the figure was a very fine looking person with white skin, sharp features, and very large eyes.

Then, from within Sri Ramakrishna's heart, there came a voice that said "*Ishamasi*[1] the Christ, the great yogi, the loving Son of God and one with the Father who gave his heart's blood and put up with endless torture in order to deliver *Jivas* [mortals] from sorrow and misery!" That figure of Jesus Christ approached Sri Ramakrishna, embraced him, and entered into him until the two became merged.

Though he had always been drawn to Jesus Christ and had a picture of Him in his room, from this vision Sri Ramakrishna became completely convinced Jesus Christ was also an Incarnation of God.[2] This vision verified

[1] *Ishamasi*, or *Sri Isa*, are the Indian names of Jesus Christ.

[2] Both Sri Ramakrishna and Jesus Christ declared themselves to be Incarnations of God. From those early days many even worshipped Sri Ramakrishna as the very embodiment of divinity — as Sri Krishna, or even Jesus Christ in another form. The following incident is recorded in *The Gospel of Sri Ramakrishna*, Nikhilananda, S., translator, p. 922. New York: 1942. The date is October 31, Saturday, 1885.

It was about eleven o'clock in the morning. Sri Ramakrishna was sitting in his room with the devotees. He was talking to a Christian devotee named Misra. Misra was born of a Christian family in

devotion to Jesus Christ as a pathway to God-realization.

As a typical Hindu, Sri Ramakrishna had deep regard for all the religions of the world. His life is a demonstration from direct experience that the different religions of the world are all pathways to the one Supreme Goal.

Jesus Christ and Sri Ramakrishna both taught in very simple language from their inner experience, without depending on any formal education. They lived lives of complete renunciation, never caring for earthly pleasures or possessions. Their sole concern was with the fulfillment of the mission for which they came to this world.

northwestern India and belonged to the Quaker sect. He was thirty-five years old. Though clad in European dress, he wore the ochre cloth of a *sannyasi* [Hindu monastic] under his foreign clothes. Two of his brothers had died on the day fixed for the marriage of one of them, and on that very day Misra had renounced the world.

MISRA: "It is Rama alone who dwells in all beings."

Sri Ramakrishna said to the younger Naren, within Misra's hearing: "Rama is one, but He has a thousand names. He who is called 'God' by the Christians is addressed by the Hindus as Rama, Krishna, Isvara, and by other names. A lake has many *ghats* [bathing places]. The Hindus drink water at one ghat and call it 'jal'; the Christians at another, and call it 'water'; the Mussalmans at a third, and call it 'pani.' Likewise, He who is God to the Christians is Allah to the Mussalmans."

MISRA: "Jesus is not the son of Mary. He is God Himself. *(To the devotees)* Now he *(pointing to Sri Ramakrishna)* is as you see him — again, he is God Himself. You are not able to recognize him. I have seen him before, in visions, though I see him now directly with my eyes. I saw a garden where he was seated on a raised seat . . .

MASTER: "Do you see visions?"

MISRA: "Sir, even when I lived at home I used to see light. Then I had a vision of Jesus. How can I describe that beauty? How insignificant is the beauty of a woman compared with that beauty!"

In the teachings of Sri Ramakrishna and Jesus Christ we find very striking similarities. Both condemned lust and greed, emphasized love of God, devotion to Him, and His grace and love in return. Both stressed prayer to God in solitude, and both declare that God can be seen — that seeing God is the Supreme Goal of life. Like Jesus Christ, Sri Ramakrishna always emphasized purification of the heart, for it is the pure hearted that see God.

The differences in their messages are mainly due to the fact that they dealt with people of varied tendencies and capacities, living in different environments. When you want to teach the same truth to different types of people, you have to accommodate or adapt your teaching to the mental conditions of these different groups. To a child you teach geography or history in one way, but to a more mature person you must present the same geographic and historical facts in a different way.

The teachings of Jesus Christ deal particularly with the way of life, and emphasize ethical principles. Sri Ramakrishna dealt more with spiritual disciplines and the goal of God-realization. Their handling of spiritual precepts differs, but there is no essential difference in the inner spirit of their words and actions.

The teachings of these great spiritual leaders were given directly to their monastic disciples and intimate devotees. Jesus Christ had twelve disciples, while Sri Ramakrishna had sixteen. But Jesus Christ also taught large numbers of people at one time, so His presentation naturally had to be well suited to the mental conditions of these people.

Jesus Christ set a very high moral tone in His sermons, and often spoke of the commandments and of ethical principles. Though He dealt with these much more than Sri Ramakrishna did, still His aim was to lead people from ethical life to the spiritual life. When the young man came running to Jesus, saying he had observed all the commandments and asking what he should do to inherit eternal life, Jesus said:

> One thing thou lackest: go thy way, sell whatsoever thou hast, and give to the poor, and thou shalt have treasure in heaven: and come, take up the cross, and follow me.
>
> (St. Mark 10:21)

So the main concern of Jesus Christ was a person's spiritual life, and not the ethical life. But many people at that time were not competent to follow the spiritual course until they became established in ethical principles, so Jesus emphasized these accordingly.

We find many parables used throughout His sermons to illustrate these principles. People are more receptive to being taught, and more likely to understand, when great truths are presented in the form of a simple story or fable. In St. Luke (8:10) Jesus tells His disciples:

> Unto you it is given to know the mysteries of the kingdom of God: but to others in parables; that seeing they might not see, and hearing they might not understand.

Through parables persons at many different levels of understanding can benefit from the teachings of Jesus Christ, without being turned away by a message which might otherwise be beyond their comprehension.

Most great spiritual teachers have used parables to convey their highest truths. Sri Ramakrishna used many stories and parables to better impart his teachings. He told the following story about the root of all troubles.

In a certain place on a river, the fishermen were catching fish, when a kite [bird] swooped down and snatched a fish. At the sight of the fish, about a thousand crows chased the kite and made a great noise with their cawing.

Whichever way the kite flew with the fish, the crows followed it. The kite flew to the south and the crows followed it there. The kite flew to the north and still the crows followed after it. The kite went east and west, but with the same result. As the kite began to fly about in confusion, lo, the fish dropped from its mouth. The crows at once let the kite alone and flew after the fish.

Thus relieved of its worries, the kite sat on the branch of a tree and thought: 'That wretched fish was at the root of all my troubles. I have now got rid of it and therefore I am at peace.'

As long as a man has the fish, that is, worldly desires, he must perform actions and consequently suffer from worry, anxiety, and restlessness. No sooner does he renounce these desires than his activities fall away and he enjoys peace in his soul.[1]

Sri Ramakrishna and Jesus Christ came to turn people's minds from the transitory to the eternal. But in spite of constant cares, worries, and sufferings, people cling to their worldly desires, content to ignore the great saviors who would bring them peace.

[1] *Tales and Parables of Sri Ramakrishna,* published by Sri Ramakrishna Math, pp. 17-18. Mylapore - Madras: 1967.

Many miracles are recorded in the life of Jesus Christ. He, like Sri Ramakrishna, did not put much stress on miracles. It was with great reluctance that He performed them.

Yet he did so because there were people who could not otherwise believe in His spiritual power and divine nature. In order to convey to people that He had true divine power, He had to show signs.

> Except ye see signs and wonders, ye will not believe. If I do not the works of my Father, believe me not.
> But if I do, though ye believe not me, believe the works: that ye may know, and believe, that the Father is in me, and I in him.   (St. John 4:48; 10:37-38)

Most people do not understand spirituality as it is, so Jesus had to convince them of His Divine spiritual nature by removing physical afflictions, bringing persons back from death, and many other miraculous incidents.

Surprisingly, those who cared for such signs did not have much faith in Christ. "But though he had done so many miracles before them, yet they believed not on him." (St. John 12:37) Jesus Christ knew that miracles do not help one's spirituality. Persons who are not spiritually developed can sometimes even perform miracles.

If you are fed with two oranges produced out of thin air your hunger is gone, but that does not help you spiritually. And you will be hungry again. It does not remove darkness from your heart, or free you from inner weakness.

The question is how far those people who participated in the fruits of the miracles were spiritually benefited. Jesus

Christ did not come to give persons physical food or to heal physical ailments. He came to lead people from the ethical level to the highest spiritual goal.

To those who sailed to Capernaum to find Him after the miracle of the loaves and the fishes, Jesus said:

> Verily, verily, I say unto you, Ye seek me, not because ye saw the miracles, but because ye did eat of the loaves, and were filled.
>
> Labour not for the meat which perisheth, but for that meat which endureth unto everlasting life, which the Son of man shall give unto you: for him hath God the Father sealed.
>
> (St. John 6:26-27)

They sought Jesus Christ because He satisfied their spiritual hunger. Jesus' greatest power is in His ability to transform a person's inner spiritual nature.

Jesus Christ and Sri Ramakrishna both came for the removal of all suffering, sins, and bondages; the removal of all darkness and delusion. They came to lead human beings to eternal life and blessedness.

The life of Sri Ramakrishna is different because the people that were close to him did not look for his divinity in miraculous signs. They understood what the spiritual ideal means, and did not have to be convinced through miracles.

Still, in the life of Sri Ramakrishna we find a few miracles, though not as many as in the life of Jesus Christ. On one occasion Sri Ramakrishna and four close devotees had gone by boat to Calcutta to visit another devotee who was ill. On the boat ride back they were all very hungry, so they stopped the boat to get something to eat.

They had very little money with them, only a few pennies in their pockets. So one of the party took what money they had and went from the boat to purchase something to eat. He bought a few sweet things, which he brought back to Sri Ramakrishna in a small leaf cup.

While the others were looking at him, Sri Ramakrishna ate the whole thing. They were all very hungry, but he did not give a single piece to any of them. Then he drank some water from the Ganges, and immediately all felt their hunger vanish completely!

There were a few other miracles in his life, but like Jesus Christ, Sri Ramakrishna did not think very highly of them. We find that both of them came particularly for the inner transformation of human beings. Sri Ramakrishna too had the power to change one's whole inner nature. By his words, by a touch, or by his very wish — he could perform that kind of miracle. There cannot be a greater miracle than this inner spiritual transformation.

Sri Ramakrishna dealt mostly with spiritual disciplines and spiritual realization because the age in which he lived particularly needed that. This age of agnosticism, atheism, and scepticism needed a demonstration of the truth of God. Without turning to any book account he had true, direct vision of God.

Sri Ramakrishna approached God with a scientific attitude — if God is real, He must be a fact of experience. So he turned to God Himself through many different forms, and had that vision of God, that direct experience. His life is a complete demonstration of God-realization: not only is

God real and has many forms and aspects, but a man can realize Him in any of these aspects.

If a person can realize God in one particular aspect, for example as Jesus Christ, he can know the true nature of God. If you take several pictures of your house from different angles, each picture will be different. No picture gives you a full view of the house; still every picture represents the entire house.

Similarly, according to one's inner development a man can conceive of God in many different ways. But each conception of God is capable of leading to God Himself.

You may worship God as the Divine Mother, Divine Father, through Jesus Christ, Sri Ramakrishna, or countless other forms and aspects. But through any of these ways you can realize God Himself — God as He is. This is the one great truth that Sri Ramakrishna taught in his life.

We find in the lives of Jesus Christ and Sri Ramakrishna many striking similarities. Though Sri Ramakrishna emphasized particularly the goal of life, and Jesus Christ the way of life, there is no fundamental difference between them. The inner spirit of their words and deeds is the same. They came in different ages to minister to the needs of different peoples. They both came to lead human beings to the one Supreme Goal.

CHAPTER V

Christ, the Messenger

by
Swami Vivekananda
(A lecture delivered at Los Angeles, California in 1900)

THE wave rises on the ocean and there is a hollow. Again another wave rises, perhaps bigger than the former to fall down again; similarly again to rise — driving onward. In the march of events, we notice the rise and fall, and we generally look toward the rise, forgetting the fall.

But both are necessary, and both are great. This is the nature of the universe. Whether in the world of our thoughts, the world of our relations in society, or in our spiritual affairs, the same movement of succession, of rises and falls, is going on.

Hence great predominances in the march of events, the liberal ideals, are marshalled ahead, to sink down, to digest, as it were — to ruminate over the past — to adjust, to conserve, to gather strength once more for a rise and a bigger rise.

The history of nations, also, has ever been like that. The great soul, the Messenger we are to study, came at a period of the history of his race which we may well designate as a great fall. We catch only little glimpses here and there of the stray records that have been kept of his sayings and doings; for verily it has been well said, that the doings and sayings of that great soul would fill the world if they had all been written down.

And the three years of his ministry were like one compressed, concentrated age, which it has taken nineteen hundred years to unfold, and who knows how much longer it will yet take!

Little men like you and me are simply the recipients of just a little energy. A few minutes, a few hours, a few years at best, are enough to spend it all, to stretch it out to its fullest strength, and then we are gone forever.

But mark this giant that came; centuries and ages pass, yet the energy that he left upon the world is not yet stretched, nor yet expended to its full. It goes on adding new vigour as the ages roll on.

Now what you see in the life of Christ is the life of all the past. It comes to him through heredity, through surroundings, through education, through his own reincarnation — the past of the race. In a manner, the past of the earth, the past of the whole world is there, upon every soul.

What are we, in the present, but a result, an effect, in the hands of that infinite past? What are we but floating wavelets in the eternal current of events, irresistibly moved forward and onward and incapable of rest?

You and I are only little things, bubbles. But there are always some giant waves in the ocean of affairs. In you and me the life of the past race has been embodied only a little; but there are giants who embody almost the whole of the past, and who stretch out their hands for the future.

These are the sign-posts, here and there, which point to the march of humanity; these are verily gigantic, their shadows covering the earth. They stand undying, eternal! As it has been said by the same Messenger: "No man hath seen God at any time, but through the Son." And that is true. Where shall we see God but in the Son?

It is true that you and I, and the poorest of us, the meanest even, embody that God, even reflect that God. The vibration of light is everywhere, omnipresent; but we have to strike the light of the lamp before we can see the light.

The Omnipresent God of the universe cannot be seen until He is reflected by these giant lamps of the earth — the Prophets, the man-Gods, the Incarnations, the embodiments of God.

We all know that God exists, and yet we do not see Him, we do not understand Him. Take one of these great Messengers of light, compare his character with the highest ideal of God that you have ever formed, and you will find that your God falls short of the ideal, that the character of the Prophet exceeds your conceptions.

You cannot even form a higher ideal of God than what the actually embodied have practically realized, and set before us as an example. Is it wrong, therefore, to worship these as God? Is it a sin to fall at the feet of these man-Gods, and worship them as the only divine beings in the world? If they are really, actually, higher than all our conceptions of

God, what harm is there in worshipping them? Not only is there no harm, but it is the only possible and positive way of worship.

However much you may try, by struggle, by abstraction, by whatsoever method you like, still so long as you are a man in the world of men, your world is human, your religion is human, and your God is human. And that must be so.

Who is not practical enough to take up an actually existing thing, and give up an idea which is only an abstraction, which he cannot grasp, and is difficult of approach except through a concrete medium? Therefore, these Incarnations of God have been worshipped in all ages and in all countries.

We are now going to study a little of the life of Christ, the Incarnation of the Jews. When Christ was born, the Jews were in that state which I call a state of fall between two waves; a state of conservatism, a state where the human mind is tired for the time being of moving forward, and is taking care only of what it has already; a state when the attention is more bent upon particulars, upon details, than the great, general and bigger problems of life; a state of stagnation, rather than a towing ahead; a state of suffering more than of doing.

Mark you, I do not blame this state of things; we have no right to criticize it. Because had it not been for this fall, the next rise, which was embodied in Jesus of Nazareth, would have been impossible. The Pharisees and Sadducees might have been insincere; they might have been doing things which they ought not to have done; they might have been even hypocrites. But whatever they were, these factors were the very cause, of which the Messenger was the effect. The Pharisees and Sadducees at one end were the very impetus, which came out at the other end, as the gigantic brain of Jesus of Nazareth.

The attention to forms, to formulas, to the everyday details of religion, and to rituals, may sometimes be laughed at; but nevertheless, within them is strength. Many times in the rushing forward we lose much strength. As a fact the fanatic is stronger than the liberal man.

Even the fanatic, therefore, has one great virtue — he conserves energy — a tremendous amount of it. As with the individual, so with the race. Energy is gathered to be conserved.

Hemmed in all around by external enemies, driven to focus in a center by the Romans, by the Hellenic tendencies in the world of intellect, by waves from Persia, India and Alexandria — hemmed in physically, mentally, and morally, there stood the race with an inherent, conservative, tremendous strength, which their descendants have not lost even today.

And the race was forced to concentrate and focus all its energies upon Jerusalem and Judaism; and, like all power when once gathered, it cannot remain collected, it must expend and expand itself. There is no power on earth which can be kept long confined within a narrow limit. It cannot be kept compressed too long to allow of expansion at a subsequent period.

This concentrated energy amongst the Jewish race found its expression at the next period in the rise of Christianity. The gathered streams collected into a body. Gradually, all the little streams joined together, and became a surging wave on the top of which, we find standing out the character of Jesus of Nazareth.

Thus every Prophet is a creation of his own times; the creation of the past of his race. He, himself, is the creator of the future. The cause of today is the effect of the past and the cause for the future.

In this position stands the Messenger. In him is embodied all that is the best and greatest in his own race; the meaning, the life for which that race has struggled for ages. And he, himself, is the impetus for the future, not only to his own race but to unnumbered other races of the world.

We must bear another fact in mind: that my view of the great Prophet of Nazareth would be from the standpoint of the Orient. Many times you forget, also, that the Nazarene himself was an Oriental of Orientals. With all your attempts to paint him with blue eyes and yellow hair, the Nazarene was still an Oriental.

All the similes, the imageries, in which the Bible is written — the scenes, the locations, the attitudes, the groups, the poetry and symbol — speak to you of the Orient: of the bright sky, of the heat, of the sun, of the desert, of the thirsty men and animals; of men and women coming with pitchers on their heads to fill them at the wells; of the flocks, of the ploughmen, of the cultivation that is going on around; of the watermill and wheel, of the mill-pond, of the millstones —all these are to be seen today in Asia.

The voice of Asia has been the voice of religion. The voice of Europe is the voice of politics. Each is great in its own sphere. The voice of Europe is the voice of ancient Greece. To the Greek mind, his immediate society was all in all. Beyond that, it is Barbarian; none but the Greek has the right to live.

Whatever the Greeks do is right and correct; whatever else there exists in the world is neither right nor correct, nor should be allowed to live. It is intensely human in its sympathies, intensely natural, intensely artistic, therefore.

The Greek lives entirely in this world. He does not care to dream. Even his poetry is practical. His gods and goddesses are not only human beings, but intensely human, with all human passions and feelings almost the same as with any of us. He loves what is beautiful, but mind you, it is always external nature: the beauty of the hills, of the snows, of the flowers; the beauty of forms and of figures; the beauty in the human face, and more often, in the human form — that is what the Greeks liked. And the Greeks being the teachers of all subsequent Europeanism, the voice of Europe is Greek.

There is another type in Asia. Think of that vast, huge continent, whose mountain tops go beyond the clouds, almost touching the canopy of heaven's blue; a rolling desert of miles upon miles, where a drop of water cannot be found, neither will a blade of grass grow; interminable forests, and gigantic rivers rushing down into the sea.

In the midst of all these surroundings, the Oriental love

of the beautiful and the sublime developed itself in another direction. It looked inside, and not outside.

There is also the thirst for Nature; and there is the same thirst for power; there is also the thirst for excellence, the same idea of the Greek and Barbarian; but it has extended over a huger circle.

We are all Christians; we are all Muslims, we are all Hindus, or all Buddhists. No matter if a Buddhist is a Chinaman, or is a man from Persia, they think that they are brothers because of their professing the same religion. Religion is the tie, the unity of humanity.

And then again the Oriental, for the same reason, is a visionary, a born dreamer. The ripples of the waterfalls, the songs of the birds, the beauties of the sun and moon and the stars and the whole earth, are pleasant enough; but they are not sufficient for the Oriental mind. He wants to dream a dream beyond.

He wants to go beyond the present. The present, as it were, is nothing to him. The Orient has been the cradle of the human race for ages, and all the vicissitudes of fortune are there. Kingdoms succeeding kingdoms; empires succeeding empires; human power, glory and wealth, all rolling down there, a Golgotha of power, and learning. That is the Orient: a Golgotha of power; of kingdoms; of learning.

No wonder the Oriental mind looks with contempt upon the things of this world, and naturally wants to see something that changeth not, which dieth not, something which in the midst of this world of misery and death is eternal, blissful, undying. An Oriental Prophet never tires of insisting upon these ideas; and, as for Prophets, you may also remember that without one exception, all the Messengers were Orientals.

We see, therefore, in the life of this great Messenger of life, the first watchword: "Not this life, but something higher." And like the true son of the Orient, he is practical in that.

You people of the West are practical in your own department, in military affairs, and in managing political circles and other things. Perhaps, the Oriental is not practical in those ways, but he is practical in his own field: he is practical in religion.

If one preaches a philosophy, tomorrow there are hundreds who will struggle their best to make it practical in their lives. If a man preaches that standing on one foot would lead to salvation, he will immediately get five hundred to stand on one foot. You may call it ludicrous; but mark you, beneath that is their philosophy — that intense practicality.

In the West, plans of salvation mean intellectual gymnastics, plans which are never worked out, never brought into practical life. In the West, the preacher who talks the best is the greatest preacher.

So in the first place we find Jesus of Nazareth, the true son of the Orient, intensely practical. He has no faith in this evanescent world and all its belongings. No need of text-torturing, as is the fashion in the West in modern times, no need of stretching out texts until they will not stretch any more. Texts are not india-rubber, and even that has its limits.

No, no making of religion to pander to the sense vanity of the present day! Mark you, let us all be honest. If we cannot follow the ideal, let us confess our weakness, but not degrade it; let not any try to pull it down.

One gets sick at heart at the different accounts of the life of the Christ that Western people give. I do not know what he was or what he was not! One would make him a great politician; another, perhaps, would make of him a great military general; another, a great patriotic Jew, and so on. Is there any warrant in the books for all such assumptions? The best commentary on the life of a great Teacher is his own life.

"The foxes have holes, the birds of the air have nests, but the Son of Man hath not where to lay His head." That is what Christ says is the only way to salvation; he lays down no other way. Let us confess in sackcloth and ashes that we cannot do that. We still have fondness for "me" and "mine." We want property, money, wealth. Woe unto us!

Let us confess and not put to shame that great Teacher of Humanity! He had no family ties. But do you think that that Man had any physical ideas in him? Do you think that this mass of light, this God and not-man, came down to earth to be the brother of animals?

And yet people make him preach all sorts of things. He had no sex ideas! He was a soul! Nothing but a soul, just working a body for the good of humanity; and that was all his relation to the body. In the soul there is no sex. The disembodied soul has no relationship to the animal, no relationship to the body.

The ideal may be far away beyond us. But never mind, keep to the ideal. Let us confess that it is our ideal, but we cannot approach it yet.

He had no other occupation in life, no other thought except that one — that he was a Spirit. He was a disembodied, unfettered, unbound Spirit. And not only so, but he, with his marvelous vision, had found that every man and woman, whether Jew or Gentile, whether rich or poor, whether saint or sinner, was the embodiment of the same undying Spirit as himself. Therefore the one work his whole life showed, was calling upon them to realize their own spiritual nature.

Give up, he says, these superstitious dreams that you are low and that you are poor. Think not that you are trampled over. Never be trampled upon; never never be tyrannized over; never be troubled; never be killed. You are all Sons of God, Immortal Spirit. "Know," he declared, "the Kingdom of Heaven is within you." "I and my Father are one."

Dare you stand up and say not only that "I am the Son of God," but I shall also find in my heart of hearts that "I and my Father are one?" That was what Jesus of Nazareth said.

He never talks of this world and of this life. He has nothing to do with it, except that he wants to get hold of the world as it is, give it a push and drive it forward and onward until the whole world has reached to the effulgent Light of God; until everyone has realized his spiritual nature, until death is vanquished and misery banished.

We have read the different stories that have been written about him. We know the scholars and their writings, and the higher criticism; and we know all that has been done by study. We are not here to discuss how much of the New Testament is true; we are not here to discuss how much of that life is historical. It does not matter at all whether the New Testament was written within five hundred years of his birth; nor does it matter, even, how much of that life is true.

But there is something behind it, something we want to imitate. To tell a lie you have to imitate a truth, and that truth is a fact. You cannot imitate that which never existed. You cannot imitate that which you never perceived.

There must have been a nucleus, a tremendous power that came down; a marvelous manifestation of spiritual power — and of that we are speaking. It stands there. Therefore we are not afraid of all the criticism of the scholars.

If I, as an Oriental, have to worship Jesus of Nazareth, there is only one way left to me; that is, to worship him as God and nothing else. Have we no right to worship him in that way, do you mean to say? If we bring him down to our own level and simply pay him a little respect as a great man, why should we worship at all?

Our Scriptures say, "These great children of Light, who manifest the Light themselves, who are Light themselves, they being worshipped, become as one with us, and we become one with them."

For, you see, in three ways man perceives God: at first the undeveloped intellect of the uneducated man sees God as far away, up in the heavens somewhere, sitting on a throne as a great Judge. He looks upon Him as a fire, as a terror.

Now, that is good, for there is nothing bad in it. You must remember that humanity travels not from error to truth, but from truth to truth. It may be, if you like it better, from lower truth to higher truth; but never from error to truth.

Suppose you start from here and travel towards the sun in a straight line. From here the sun looks only small in size. Suppose you go forward a million miles, the sun will be much bigger. At every stage the sun will become bigger and bigger.

Suppose twenty thousand photographs had been taken of the same sun from different standpoints; these twenty thousand photographs will all certainly differ from one another. But can you deny that each is a photograph of the same sun?

So all forms of religion, high or low, are just different stages toward that eternal state of Light, which is God Himself. Some embody a lower view, some a higher, and that is all the difference. Therefore the religions of the unthinking masses all over the world must be, and have always been, of a God who is outside of the universe; who lives in heaven; who governs from that place; who is a punisher of the bad and a rewarder of the good, and so on.

As man advanced spiritually he began to feel that God was omnipresent, that He must be in him, that He must be everywhere; that He was not a distant God, but clearly the Soul of all souls. As my soul moves my body, even so is God the mover of my soul. Soul within soul.

And a few individuals who had developed enough and were pure enough, went still further, and at last found God.

As the New Testament says: "Blessed are the pure in heart, for they shall see God." And they found at last, that they and the Father were one.

You find that all these three stages are taught by the Great Teacher in the New Testament. Note the Common Prayer he taught: "Our Father which art in Heaven, hallowed be Thy name," and so on. A simple prayer, a child's prayer; and mark you, it is the "Common Prayer" because it is intended for the uneducated masses.

To a higher circle, to those who had advanced a little more, he gave a more elevated teaching: "I am in my Father, and ye in me, and I in you." Do you remember that?

And then, when the Jews asked him who he was, he declared that he and his Father were one, and the Jews thought that that was blasphemy. What did he mean by that? This has been also told by your old Prophets: "Ye are gods and all of you are children of the Most High."

Mark the same three stages; you will find that it is easier for you to begin with the first and end with the last.

The Messenger came to show the path: that the Spirit is not in forms; that it is not through all sorts of vexatious and knotty problems of philosophy that you know the Spirit. Better that you had no learning, better that you never read a book in your life. These are not at all necessary for salvation; neither wealth, nor position, nor power, not even learning.

But what is necessary is that one thing, purity: "Blessed are the pure in heart," for the Spirit in its own nature is pure. How can it be otherwise? It is of God; it has come from God. In the language of the Bible, "It is the breath of God;" in the language of the Koran, "It is the soul of God."

Do you mean to say that the Spirit of God can ever be impure? But alas, it has been, as it were, covered over with the dust and dirt of ages, through our own actions, good and evil. Various works which were not correct, which were not true, have covered the same Spirit with the dust and dirt of the ignorance of ages.

It is only necessary to clear away the dust and dirt, and then the Spirit shines immediately. "Blessed are the pure in heart for they shall see God." "The Kingdom of Heaven is within you." Where goest thou to seek for the Kingdom of God? asks Jesus of Nazareth, when it is there, within you. Cleanse the Spirit, and it is there. It is already yours.

How can you get what is not yours? It is yours by right. You are the heirs of immortality, sons of the Eternal Father.

This is the great lesson of the Messenger, and another which is the basis of all religions —is renunciation. How can you make the Spirit pure? By renunciation.

A rich young man asked Jesus, "Good Master, what shall I do that I may inherit eternal life? And Jesus said unto him, One thing that thou lackest: go thy way, sell whatsoever thou hast, and give to the poor, and thou shalt have treasures in heaven: and come, take up thy cross, and follow Me. And he was sad at that saying, and went away grieved: for he had great possessions."

We are all more or less like that. The Voice is ringing in our ears day and night. In the midst of our pleasures and joys, in the midst of worldly things, we think that we have forgotten everything else. Then comes a moment's pause and the Voice rings in our ears: "Give up all that thou hast and follow Me;" Whosoever will save his life shall lose it; and whosoever shall lose his life for My sake shall find it."

For whoever gives up this life for His namesake, finds the life immortal. In the midst of all our weakness there is a moment of pause and the Voice rings: "Give up all that thou hast; give it to the poor and follow Me." This is the one ideal he preaches, and this has been the ideal preached by all the great Prophets of the world: renunciation.

What is meant by renunciation? That there is only one ideal in morality: unselfishness. Be selfless. The ideal is perfect unselfishness. When a man is struck on the right cheek, he turns the left also. When a man's coat is carried off, he gives away his cloak also.

We should work in the best way we can, without dragging the ideal down. Here is the ideal. When a man has no more self in him, no possession, nothing to call "me" or "mine;" has given himself up entirely, destroyed himself as it were — in that man is God Himself — for in him self-will is gone, crushed out, annihilated. That is the ideal man.

We cannot reach that state yet. But let us worship the ideal, and slowly struggle to reach that ideal, though it may be with faltering steps. It may be tomorrow, or it may be a thousand years hence, but that ideal has to be reached. For it is not only the end, but also the means. To be unselfish, perfectly selfless, is salvation itself, for the man within dies, and God alone remains.

One more point. All the teachers of humanity are unselfish. Suppose Jesus of Nazareth was teaching, and a man came and told him: "What you teach is beautiful; I believe that it is the way to perfection and I am ready to follow it; but I do not care to worship you as the only begotten Son of God."

What would be the answer of Jesus of Nazareth? "Very well, brother, follow the ideal and advance in your own way. I do not care whether you give me the credit for the teaching or not. I am not a shopkeeper. I do not trade in religion. I only teach truth, and truth is nobody's property. Nobody can patent truth. Truth is God Himself. Go forward."

But what the disciples say nowadays is: "No matter whether you practice the teachings or not, do you give credit to the Man? If you credit the Master, you will be saved; if not, there is no salvation for you."

And thus the whole teaching of the Master is degenerated, and all the struggle and fight is for the personality of the Man. They do not know that in imposing that difference they are, in a manner, bringing shame to the very Man they want to honor, the very Man that would have shrunk with shame from such an idea. What did he care if there was one man in the world that remembered him or not? He had to deliver his message, and he gave it.

And if he had twenty thousand lives he would give them all up for the poorest man in the world. If he had to be tortured millions of times, for a million despised Samaritans, and if for each one of them the sacrifice of his own life would be the only condition of salvation, he would have given his life. And all this without wishing to have his name known even to a single person. Quiet, unknown, silent, would he work, just as the Lord works.

Now what would the disciple say? He will tell you that you may be a perfect man, perfectly unselfish, but unless you give the credit to our Teacher, to our Saint, it is of no avail. Why? What is the origin of this superstition, this ignorance?

The disciple thinks that the Lord can manifest Himself only once. There lies the whole mistake. God manifests Himself to you in man.

But throughout Nature, what happens once must have happened before, and must happen in the future. There is nothing in Nature which is not bound by law, and that means that whatever happens once, must go on and must have been going on.

In India they have the same idea of the Incarnations of God. One of their great Incarnations, Krishna — whose grand Sermon the *Bhagavad Gita* some of you might have read — says: "Though I am unborn, of changeless nature and Lord of beings, yet subjugating My Prakriti [primordial nature], I come into being by My own Maya [divine power]. Whenever virtue subsides and immorality prevails, then I body Myself forth. For the protection of the good, for the destruction of the wicked, and for the establishment of Dharma, I come into being in every age." Whenever the world goes down, the Lord comes to help it forward; and so He does from time to time and place to place.

In another passage He speaks to this effect: Wherever thou findest a great soul of immense power and purity struggling to raise humanity, know that he is born of My splendor, that I am there working through him.

Let us, therefore, find God not only in Jesus of Nazareth but in all the great Ones that have preceded him, in all that came after him, and all that are yet to come. Our worship is unbounded and free. They are all manifestations of the same Infinite God. They are all pure and unselfish; they struggled, and gave up their lives for us, poor human beings. They each and all suffer vicarious atonement for every one of us, and also for all that are to come hereafter.

In a sense you are all Prophets; every one of you is a Prophet, bearing the burden of the world on your own shoulders. Have you ever seen a man, have you ever seen a woman, who is not quietly, patiently bearing his or her little burden of life?

The great Prophets were giants — they bore a gigantic world on their shoulders. Compared with them we are pigmies, no doubt, yet we are doing the same task. In our little circles, in our little homes we are bearing our little crosses. There is no one so evil, no one so worthless, but he has to bear his own cross.

But with all our mistakes, with all our evil thoughts and evil deeds, there is a bright spot somewhere; there is still somewhere the golden thread through which we are always in touch with the divine. For know for certain, that the moment the touch of the divine is lost, there would be annihilation. And because none can be annihilated, there is always somewhere in our heart of hearts, however low and degraded we may be, a little circle of light which is in constant touch with the divine.

Our salutations go to all the past Prophets, whose

teachings and lives we have inherited, whatever might have been their race, clime or creed! Our salutations go to all those God-like men and women, who are working to help humanity, whatever be their birth, color, or race! Our salutations to those who are coming in the future — living Gods — to work unselfishly for our descendants!

CHAPTER VI

The Kingdom of God
is Within You

ESUS Christ began His preaching with an announce-
ment of the coming of the Kingdom of God:

The time is fulfilled, and the kingdom of God is at hand:
repent ye, and believe the Gospel.   (St. Mark 1:15)

We find the expressions "Kingdom of God" and
"Kingdom of Heaven" used synonymously throughout the
New Testament. St. Matthew used "Kingdom of Heaven,"
while the other three Gospel writers used "Kingdom of
God."

Even before Jesus Christ, John the Baptist preached:
"Repent ye: for the Kingdom of Heaven is at hand." (St.
Matt. 3:2) And long before John the Baptist, the Jewish
prophets, particularly Isaiah and Daniel, preached about
the Kingdom of God.

The origin of the idea of the Kingdom of God can be
traced to Jewish theocratic belief, and to the political
condition of Palestine. For centuries Palestine had been

over-run by foreign aggressors. On one hand the Assyrians, Hittites, and Babylonians carried their campaigns against Palestine from the East; and on the other, the Egyptians, Greeks, and Romans made military inroads to the very heart of Palestine from the West. The Jewish people found themselves helpless against these powerful foreign invaders.

When earthly help fails, we generally lift our thoughts to the highest, we raise our hands in supplication to the Divine Power. This the Jewish people did: they prayed to the Lord that He would intervene in human affairs and send His Messiah to free Palestine from the grip of foreigners.

They prayed He would establish His kingdom upon the earth, where all would follow the path of righteousness; where Divine Will would govern the political and social life of the people; and where all want and misery would disappear. That was the belief among the Jews, and their prophets kept this belief alive.

Therefore when Jesus Christ came, the idea of such an earthly kingdom was predominant in the minds of the Jewish people. His use of the phrase "Kingdom of God" met with every possibility of getting a ready response from His people. Using Jewish terms, He conveyed a very profound truth, though His idea of this Kingdom was different from that of the Jewish people.

According to the Jewish belief, the Kingdom of Heaven was actually to be an earthly kingdom. They imagined a paradise on earth with a theocratic government, where a representative of the Lord, such as David, would rule.

Jesus Christ has not used the phrase in exactly the same

sense. In fact it appears that He used the expression "Kingdom of God," or "Kingdom of Heaven," in three different senses.

First, in some places Jesus has expressed the popular conception of a kingdom on earth.

Secondly, He used it in the sense of the abode of God, or Heaven.

And the third sense is that of God-consciousness, a state of full spiritual awareness.

Jesus particularly stressed the last two: the sense of the abode of God, where the righteous and devoted find access; and in the sense of God-consciousness.

In the first sense, there is a reference to an earthly kingdom in the second line of the Lord's Prayer: "Thy kingdom come. Thy will be done, on earth, as it is in Heaven." And in St. Matthew (25:34):

> Then shall the King say unto them on his right hand, Come, ye blessed of my Father, inherit the kingdom prepared for you from the foundation of the world.

Here Jesus concedes to the popular view of an earthly Kingdom of God, where human beings will live in happiness and peace.

Great teachers such as Jesus Christ Himself have declared that they come not to destroy, but to fulfill. They do not pull the ground from under the feet of the spiritual seeker, loose though the soil may be. They try to lead the seeker to firmer ground from wherever he happens to be. Sri Ramakrishna said: "Do not destroy anybody's belief. Lead him to higher and higher belief, to higher and higher conceptions of the truth."

Jesus Christ followed the same principle. Though He knew that the Kingdom of God is within an individual, He tried to lead people gradually to this truth from wherever they might be.

Jesus also acknowledges another popular view — that of the Kingdom of God as a celestial dominion. We know He is not speaking of an earthly paradise, for He states the requirements to enter the Kingdom of Heaven, and urges people to actively prepare themselves for this Kingdom.

> Lay not up for yourselves treasures upon earth, where moth and rust doth corrupt, and where thieves break through and steal:
>
> But lay up for yourselves treasures in heaven, where neither moth nor rust doth corrupt and where thieves do neither break through nor steal.   (St. Matt. 6: 19,20)
>
> Let your light so shine before men that they may see your good works and glorify your Father which is in Heaven.
>   (5:16)
>
> For I say unto you, That except your righteousness shall exceed the righteousness of the scribes and Pharises, ye shall in no case enter into the kingdom of Heaven.   (5:20)
>
> Be ye therefore perfect, even as your Father which is in Heaven is perfect.   (5:48)

Jesus Christ evidently meant a spiritual kingdom where people can go after death through faith and devotion. It is those who are virtuous, sincere, and loving to all who gain this kingdom.

In spite of this, two of Jesus' own disciples mis-understood Him. They knew that the Kingdom of Heaven would not be on this earth. But they thought it would be some celestial kingdom where men could live in happiness and plenty, and enjoy life to a greater extent than on this earth. And of course they, being disciples of Christ, should have special places of authority and respect in this kingdom. Perhaps this was in the minds of the two brother disciples:

> And James and John, the sons of Zebede, come unto him, saying, Master we would that thou shouldest do for us whatsoever we shall desire.
>
> And he said unto them, What would ye that I should do for you?
>
> They said unto him, Grant unto us that we may sit, one on thy right hand, and the other on thy left, in thy glory.
>
> But Jesus said unto them, Ye know not what ye ask: can ye drink of the cup that I drink of? and be baptized with the baptism that I am baptized with?
>
> And they said unto him, We can. And Jesus said unto them, Ye shall indeed drink of the cup that I drink of; and with the baptism that I am baptized withal shall ye be baptized:
>
> But to sit on my right hand and on my left hand is not mine to give; but it shall be given to them for whom it is prepared.
>
> (St. Mark 10:35-40)

Jesus Christ meant the abode of the Lord to which the virtuous and the pious have access, where they live in perpetual loving service to the Lord. He did not mean a place of personal glory, or for the fulfillment of sense desires, which is what the two brothers seemed to understand by the "Kingdom of Heaven."

Jesus also used this expression in the sense of God-consciousness, of experiencing God in your heart. This is His true view of the Kingdom of Heaven. He says: "The Kingdom of God cometh not with observation: Neither shall they say, Lo here! or, lo there! for, behold, the kingdom of God is within you."   (St. Luke 17:20-21)

Here, Jesus Christ rejects the common view, and declares the central truth with regard to God's Kingdom: "The Kingdom of God cometh not with observation." You cannot objectively perceive the Kingdom of Heaven; it does not exist outside yourself. It is within you.

In that God-consciousness you find the Kingdom of God wherever you are. It has no special reference to space or time, for in any place, at any time, you can enter this Kingdom of Heaven.

Another passage which corroborates this idea is found in St. Luke (9:27):

> But I tell you of a truth, there be some standing here, which shall not taste of death, till they see the kingdom of God.

Because these persons will have realized their unity with the Divine Being — which in fact already exists — then before they die they will see the Kingdom of God.

One can realize and attain that God-consciousness right here, right now. "The Kingdom of God is within you" everywhere, and at all times. No message can be more enlightening or more encouraging to the human heart than this.

Through parables, Jesus Christ took great pains trying to explain this kind of Kingdom of God. He did so because it is very difficult to think of the inner consciousness developed to such an extent that you will always be in the Kingdom of God, regardless of external conditions. This great truth is easily understood only by those who are highly spiritually advanced. In order to clarify this idea, Jesus used many parables.

> The Kingdom of heaven is like to a grain of mustard seed, which a man took, and sowed in his field:
>
> Which indeed is the least of all seeds: but when it is grown, it is the greatest among herbs, and becometh a tree, so that the birds of the air come and lodge in the branches thereof.
>
> Another parable spake he unto them; The kingdom of heaven is like unto leaven, which a woman took, and hid in three measures of meal, till the whole was leavened.
>
> (St. Matt. 13:31-33)

It is not that Divine kingdom where you go after death; it is a kingdom which begins in a very, very small degree with just a little consciousness of your relationship with the Divinity, just a little awareness of your immortal spiritual Self.

Then, just as a tiny mustard seed grows into a large tree, or a bit of yeast leavens many measures of flour, similarly this little bit of spiritual sense grows within you through spiritual discipline, until it shines forth as complete God-consciousness in the Kingdom of Heaven.

From ancient times, this very truth has been reiterated in Hinduism. In fact the whole Vedantic literature is replete with this essential spiritual principle.

Yet how is it possible that "The Kingdom of God is within you?" Can it be that this realm of eternal light, eternal life, and eternal peace is already here?

Conceived of as the highest culmination of life's journey, where death, decay, delusion, and pain in any form are unknown, is it possible that this Kingdom is right within your heart and the heart of all human beings?

If we look closely into this physical body, what do we find? We find that it is made of mortal clay, subject to birth, growth, decay and death; hunger and thirst, heat and cold. It is the abode of ailments, a bag of filth, truly speaking, however fascinating it may appear to us. Yet it is said the Kingdom of God is within a person!

And what about the condition of the mind? The mind is a playground of good and evil forces, where pain and pleasure alternate. It is ever restless, constantly assailed by cares and worries. Where is a place for the Kingdom of God within this mind?

Vedanta's age-old answer is this: man is not just a physical body, or a body-mind complex, but something beyond the body, beyond the mind. He observes the changing physical conditions and mental states, and at the same time knows himself as the observer.

Change always implies an unchanging witness. So there is, in the human system, an unchanging principle. That unchanging principle is of the nature of pure Consciousness.

You know that you are not just a physical being or a

psychophysical system, but that you are something beyond both body and mind. You exist as conscious spirit, watching the physical conditions, watching the mental conditions.

That conscious spiritual principle is at the same time self-aware, self-manifest. You never doubt your own existence, you cannot doubt it. Only a conscious being can have the ability to doubt at all. Your existence is self-manifest, self-revealing, because you are essentially pure spirit: birthless, growthless, decayless, deathless — ever the same.

That principle of Consciousness is the only constant factor in the human personality. Man's real self is pure, illumined, self-shining, and free.

Still a person may think, "So, I am essentially pure, free, eternal spirit. I am a little spirit, and God is the Supreme Spirit. I belong to Him. He is omnipotent, omniscient, and dwells in His own sphere, far from us. How can He be within me?"

This question also arises, and Vedanta declares that God is not far away from anything, He is not apart from anything. God *is* within you. Nothing exists outside Him, He includes everything. He is, in fact, the sole Reality, the essence of everything. The finest of all existences, He underlies each and every form of existence. God is the one self-effulgent Supreme Reality, lying hidden everywhere, but the very perfection of existence, self-luminous pure Consciousness.

That Reality, the Supreme Being, God, is right here within you as your inmost self. This self-evident, conscious spirit which you cannot deny, is the immediate and direct manifestation of the Supreme Spirit. You can realize this Supreme Spirit by realizing your spiritual self. To reach the Soul of the universe you first have to reach your own soul; you contact Supreme Spirit through spirit. There is no other way of direct communication with the Supreme Reality.

Underlying all forms that constantly appear and disappear, that Supreme Reality is present everywhere, but His special manifestation in this physical plane is through the psychophysical system of living creatures. Sri Krishna says in the *Bhagavad Gita,* "I am the Self dwelling in the hearts of all beings."

Vedanta says that this body is the very city of Brahman,[1] God, because in this body Brahman dwells with a retinue of physical organs — the organs of perception, the organs of action, the organ of cognition, the life principle. In this city there is a palace, the abode of Brahman, which is in the heart. It is here that the Divine Being, the omnipresent One, is self-manifest.

Thus the Supreme Consciousness, all-pervading, sustaining the universe, is manifest within the heart of each and every living creature as individualized conscious spirit.

Because of this Spirit the mind, which has no light of its own, appears to be effulgent, as if mind itself thinks, knows, feels, and imagines. The light of Consciousness is also transmitted to this physical system, so that the eyes apparently see, the hands apparently feel, and the mouth

[1]Brahman is the all-pervading transcendental Reality of Vedanta philosophy: impersonal, absolute Existence, the One without a second.

apparently speaks.[1]

Through every function of every organ, this light of Spirit is shining. Though the light of Consciousness apparently comes from the mind, it really comes from the Supreme Spirit. That alone is the source of all consciousness.

That Supreme, self-effulgent Spirit is individualized here in this body, and being identified with the psychophysical system becomes manifest as the ego.

"I am a psychophysical being."

"I live in this city."

"I like this."

"I need that."

Because you impose upon your Self the needs and urges of this physical body, you think that you have hunger and thirst, that you need a home, that you need companions, etc. All problems arise from this fact — that there is a confusion between the mind and the pure Spirit. The two have been mingled, somehow or other. Just as light coming through mist creates haziness and obscurity, similarly pure Spirit coming through the mind does not reveal itself fully.

Although you realize yourself as existent, still you do not fully realize yourself as you are. You mistakenly identify yourself with this body-mind complex, and attribute to yourself all that belongs to the body and to the mind.

.

[1]During sleep when this light recedes from the organs, the eyes cannot see, the ears cannot hear, the hands cannot grasp, the mouth cannot speak. Just a little bit of consciousness is left so autonomous functions can continue.

"Know ye not that ye are the temple of God, that the Spirit of God dwelleth within you?" (I Cor. 3:16)

This has been described in many different ways in Vedantic literature. We find in the *Kena Upanishad* (1:5), "That which the organ of speech cannot apprehend, but which apprehends the organ of speech, that is Brahman, the Supreme Reality, shining in the heart."

Do not think that God is existing somewhere beyond the highest firmament. He who you worship as existing far from you, who you worship as inaccessible, is right within your heart, ever-manifest as conscious Spirit.

"That which the mind cannot apprehend but which apprehends the mind." (Ke.Up.1:6) Are you not observing the mind, can't you see it change? You are not the mind, for the observer and the observed can not be the same.

> That which the eyes cannot see, but which perceives the eyes, because of which the eyes see; that which the ears cannot hear, but which perceives the ears, because of which the ears hear;
>
> that which the nose cannot smell, but because of which the nose has the power of smelling — know that to be the Supreme Reality, ever dwelling within you. (Ke. Up. 1:7-9)

By realizing *that* you find the Kingdom of God. You realize God as the source of all joy, of all wisdom, of all light, of all peace, of all knowledge.

There is one and only one place in the universe where man meets God. After searching in vain for God in the churches, in the forest's depths, in the mountain's heights, after scaling even the starry firmament — the mind comes back and finds God right within the heart. Here is the direct manifestation of the Supreme Spirit as spirit.

Just as every ray of light coming from the sun belongs to the sun, similarly when you realize this individual spirit, you find it belongs to the Infinite Spirit. As it is said in the *Katha Upanishad* (I:2:20):

> Finer than the finest, greater than the greatest, that Supreme Self, soul of the universe, is hidden in the hearts of living creatures. Persons free from sense desires realize that Supreme Being through the purification of the body and the mind.

When they realize that, they find the source of all joy, of all light, of all life. When they find the source within, such persons find it everywhere. They find that all the dualities and relativities of the manifold only apparently exist. Underlying all these apparent forms there is one Reality, self-effulgent, the very embodiment of purity, of strength, of wisdom and peace.

So Jesus Christ says: "Blessed are the pure in heart: for they shall see God." It is through the purification of the mind that you see God.

How is the mind purified? By following the path of righteousness. Each time you try to follow the path of virtue, you attune yourself to the Supreme Self. Our difficulty is that we have attuned our selves to the psychophysical system. By spiritual effort, we must try to attune ourselves to the Supreme Self, to which we really belong.

Each time you follow a moral principle, knowingly or unknowingly, you attune your self to the Supreme Self; you attune this finite self to the Infinite One. You turn your heart from darkness to the source of all light.

So lift your thoughts from the physical plane and meditate deeply on the spiritual self within you. If you cannot do that directly, follow the path of righteousness through faith.

As you follow this path, the light of Spirit will enter into you, because you will be attuning yourself to the Supreme Self. The antidote for darkness is light and nothing else. As the light of the Spirit enters your heart, darkness will be dispelled, weaknesses will be removed, until at last you say: "Ah, now I see! I am the observer of all physical events, I am the observer of all mental states and processes. How can I be the same as this psychophysical system? I am really pure Spirit!"

The moment you have that Spirit consciousness, you are reborn. Jesus Christ said: "Except a man be born again, he cannot see the Kingdom of God."

The constant theme of Vedanta is that "the Kingdom of God is within you," because God shines within as your inmost self. Beyond this body, beyond this mind, shines that light of Supreme Spirit: ever-effulgent, the very perfection of existence wherein no darkness or delusion of any kind can endure.

We find that Jesus Christ in simple, familiar words, has presented humanity with the deepest of spiritual truths, and He has also pointed out the means through which this truth can be realized.

CHAPTER VII

Resist not Evil

W E are all familiar with the Biblical injunction "Resist not evil." In His Sermon on the Mount, Jesus Christ said:

Ye have heard that it hath been said, An eye for an eye, and a tooth for a tooth:

But I say unto you, That ye resist not evil; but whosoever shall smite thee on thy right cheek, turn to him the other also.

And if any man will sue thee at the law, and take away thy coat, let him have thy cloak also.

And whosoever shall compel thee to go a mile, go with him twain.

Give to him that asketh thee, and from him that would borrow of thee turn not thou away.

Ye have heard that it hath been said, Thou shalt love thy neighbour, and hate thine enemy.

But I say unto you, Love your enemies, bless them that curse you, do good to them that hate you, and pray for them which despitefully use you, and persecute you. (St. Matt. 5:38-44)

By the non-resistance of evil, Jesus Christ does not mean only the passive endurance of sufferings caused by others. He means doing positive good in return for wrong. Jesus Christ, however, was not the first teacher of this sublime ethical principle.

Rabbi Hillel, the great Jewish teacher and philosopher, taught active non-resistance before Jesus' birth. Hillel came to Palestine from Babylonia, and died when Christ was nine years old.

But Rabbi Hillel cannot be called the originator of this teaching either, for nearly six hundred years before Jesus Christ, the great Chinese philosopher and teacher Lao-tse was instructing his followers "return good for evil." Though said to be fifty-three years younger than Lao-tse, the sage Confucius was also living at that time. He taught his disciples: "Do not do unto others what you do not want to be done unto you by others."

But Confucius' followers complained to him that "Lao-tse says a person should return good for evil. Now what is your opinion?"

Confucius replied: "What then will you return for good? Recompense injury with justice and return good for good."

When Lao-tse heard this he commented: "The good I meet with goodness, the bad I also meet with goodness. For virtue is goodness throughout."

At about the same time, Buddha was teaching this very principle in India.[1] It is forcefully illustrated in his Parable of the Saw:

> Yea, disciples, even if highway robbers with a two-handed saw shall take and dismember you limb by limb, whosoever grow darkened in mind thereby would not be fulfilling my injunctions.

> Even then, disciples, thus must you school yourselves; Unsullied shall our minds remain, neither shall evil word escape our lips. Kind and compassionate ever, we will abide loving of heart nor harbor secret hate.

> And those robbers will we permeate with a stream of loving thought unfailing; and forth from them proceeding, enfold and permeate the whole wide world with constant thoughts of loving kindness, ample, expanding, measureless, free from enmity, free from ill will!

> Yes, verily my disciples, thus must you school yourselves.

There cannot be a greater expression of the principle of returning good for evil. Just as a sandalwood tree hewed by a woodcutter envelops the woodcutter in its fragrance, similarly even when a person is persecuted, his compassion and love must envelop the wrong-doer.

Many centuries before Buddha, Sri Krishna taught the same ideal to his disciple Uddhava. In the *Bhagavatam* we find:

---

[1] The sixth century B.C. was a golden age in human history. In addition to Lao-tse, Confucius, and Buddha, the Greek philosopher-mathematician Pythagoras was active at this time, and the Eleatic school of Greek philosophy flourished under Xenophanes and his pupil Parmenides.

Even though scolded by the wicked, or insulted, ridiculed, calumniated, beaten, bound, robbed of his living, or spat upon, or otherwise abominably treated by the ignorant — being thus variously shaken and placed in dire extremities, the man who desires his well-being should deliver himself by his own effort [through patience and non-resistance].   (XI:22.57, 58)

This sublime ethical principle of returning good for evil is based on a very deep spiritual truth — the underlying Oneness of all. Those who develop this spiritual vision of one Reality — one Supreme Self dwelling in the hearts of all as the innermost self — find their individual self expanding and enveloping all beings.

With such spiritual insight, whom will they praise? Whom will they blame? The guilty and the innocent are seen to be one. Such persons naturally become established in the practice of returning good for evil.

Others who have not quite reached this culmination of spiritual life have to practice non-resistance with effort. What is natural for the illumined needs effort on the part of the unillumined.

All actions of an illumined soul are naturally beneficial to all living beings, for here ethical principle blends with the highest spiritual truth. There is no fundamental difference between spirituality and morality. At their roots the two become one.

In a general way, then, we can say that morality means the attunement of the individual self to the universal Self. It means getting rid of selfishness in all possible ways, because selfishness breeds all vices. No one will do harm unselfishly.

One must cultivate unselfishness by attuning oneself to the Supreme Self that enfolds all beings. This is the fundamental ethical principle. When this egoistic self becomes completely attuned to the Supreme Self, you develop the vision of one Supreme Being — holding everything, penetrating everything.

Then you know that in hurting others you hurt yourself. In helping others, you help yourself, because your self is not confined within this psychophysical system. Your self actually expands far beyond the confines of this system, and is ever united with the Supreme Self that pervades the whole universe.

A human being is essentially not something limited. We are a circle, the center of which is here in this finite consciousness, but the circumference of which is nowhere.

Apparently man is a psychophysical being: he eats, he drinks, he sleeps, he talks, he laughs, he works, he suffers, he enjoys. He is born, he grows, he decays, and dies. This is the apparent man.

But underlying this changing man, underlying all the changing conditions of the body and the mind, there is the spiritual man, the real Self of man. That spiritual man never suffers any change. Beyond birth, beyond growth, beyond death, beyond hunger, beyond virtue, beyond vice, beyond knowledge and ignorance — that spiritual Self abides within you.

When a person becomes awakened to that spiritual Self, becomes aware of the true nature of the self, he realizes that he does not actually belong to this physical universe. He belongs to that Reality that sustains and manifests all things.

So following the principle of returning good for evil ultimately leads to this highest spiritual realization. Only then does one not have to make any effort to return good for evil, for he is automatically established in it.

This human nature is geared to the Supreme Self. When you develop selflessness, you feel expanded. But the moment you have selfishness, you feel cooped-up, restricted; there is uneasiness within you. Human nature is such that there is no room for any kind of vindictiveness or hatred. No justifiable hatred should be indulged in by any human being.

The moment you have hatred, even with good reason, that hatred will hurt you before it hurts anyone else. Whenever you have ill-feeling, that ill-feeling will victimize you before it can victimize anyone else. Before your hatred reaches its target, it will attack you. You are always the first victim of your own ill-feeling.

There is no place for even righteous indignation in human life. You may indulge in it, but always at your own cost. The moment you have any kind of ill feeling towards anybody, rightly or wrongly, you are the first victim. Whenever you lose suavity of mind, that very moment your vision becomes distorted and your judgment becomes warped. Who suffers more?

St. Peter came to Jesus Christ and asked, "Lord, how oft shall my brother sin against me, and I forgive him? till seven times?"

And Jesus said to him, "I say not unto thee, Until seven times: but, Until seventy times seven." (St. Matt. 18:21,22)

There is a great psychological truth in this teaching. If you do not forgive, you are hurt. If you forgive, you gain. Though there are human weaknesses that have to be taken into account, by all means one should try to forgive as much as one can.

Without a doubt this is the highest level of ethical life, and ordinary human beings cannot easily rise to this height. Yet by persistent efforts and systematic practice, each and every individual can eventually be all-forgiving.

Broadly speaking, human beings dwell on three different planes or principles, designated by the Sanskrit words *tamas, rajas,* and *sattva.*

When *tamas* prevails, a person is generally very selfish, cowardly, and lazy. His mind is dull and lethargic, his body sluggish and weak. He lives in a state of general delusion.

At the second stage when *rajas* prevails, a person becomes energetic. He makes plans and is ambitious — he wants to achieve many things in this life. He seeks power and pleasure, and has consequent worries, fears, and troubles causing restlessness of body and mind.

When one arrives at the third stage, *sattva,* the mind becomes serene. In that serene mind true knowledge shines, true insight develops; there is real joy. Until a person develops *sattva,* he cannot have contentment or serenity in this life; he cannot have true knowledge or true happiness.

Persons who rise to the level of *sattva* have a chance of

practicing the principle of returning good for evil. But persons who are on the level of *tamas,* cowardly and indolent, cannot at once go to this level. They have to progress gradually. From the level of *tamas,* they have to rise to the level of *rajas;* they have to become active first.

A coward has to become a hero before he can be a saint, so let him cultivate the power to redress the evil in this world. It is on this platform that most people stand; human society follows the principle of reciprocity — "An eye for an eye, a tooth for a tooth."

In every country, among all nations, there are law courts, police forces, and military powers, all to return good for good, evil for evil. If you do good you will be rewarded and well-treated; if you do bad, you will be punished. This is the plane of justice, the plane of reciprocity.

A person of *tamasic* nature who is very vindictive, who will break your head if you but scratch him, cannot at once follow the principle of returning good for evil. He can only follow the principle of "tit-for-tat," "an eye for an eye, a tooth for a tooth." For him this principle is good! But do not break his head if he scratches you; just emphasize justice.

Then when such a person becomes established in the principle of justice, when he gets over his vindictiveness, then we can tell him, "Yes, it is better to forgive." By developing love for justice, gradually he will develop forgiveness. Then it may be possible for him to return good for evil.

So the person of *tamasic* nature should enter into the battle of life. By right deeds, by the performance of his duties honestly and efficiently, let him make a stand in this life. It is the hero, the courageous, active person, who can become spiritual. There is no place for escapism in spiritual life.

When a man has learned to be brave, to stand for a just cause and defend the weak, protect the virtuous, and curb the wicked, he has reached the level of *rajas*. Here he tries to achieve what we call success in life — prosperity and pleasure (by honest means, of course).

By following the path of virtue his mind gradually becomes purified, and he starts to see material values in their true light. He begins to realize the inadequacy of all worldly achievements. From the temporal, his mind turns to the eternal. Once he reaches the *sattvic* plane he becomes a seeker of spiritual ideals. Only then can a person hope to practice true non-resistance.

In this way through gradations one has to rise to the level of non-resistance of evil. Everyone cannot be expected to follow this principle at once, but everyone can be expected to rise to this level ultimately.

In the *Bhagavad Gita* we find Sri Krishna delivering this message to Arjuna: "Fight, establish your just cause, fight!" But to Uddhava in the *Bhagavatam* Sri Krishna says: "Whatever ill treatment you receive from another, you should not return evil for evil, you should return good." Why is there such a difference in Sri Krishna's teachings?

Because Uddhava was a spiritual man, on the level of *sattva,* while Arjuna was on the level of *rajas*. Arjuna was a warrior, a hero, whose duty it was to protect the virtuous and weak and to subdue the wicked.

Uddhava, on the other hand, had realized the futility of transitory pleasures and possessions. He was disillusioned with the dualities of life, and understood that in this life you cannot have life without death, youth without old age, pleasure without pain. He was ready to dedicate himself to the attainment of the spiritual Goal, the Eternal.

So for Uddhava, returning good for evil was the right ideal, but for Arjuna it was not. Swami Vivekananda very clearly expressed this distinction in his lecture "Each is Great in His Own Place":

> In reading the *Bhagavad Gita,* many of you in Western countries may have felt astonished at the second chapter, wherein when Arjuna refuses to fight or offer resistance because his adversaries were his friends and relatives, and makes the plea that non-resistance is the highest ideal of love, Sri Krishna calls him a hypocrite and a coward.
>
> There is a great lesson for us all to learn ... We must first take care to understand whether we have the power of resistance or not. Then, having the power, if we renounce it and do not resist, we are doing a grand act of love; but if we cannot resist, and yet, at the same time, try to deceive ourselves into the belief that we are actuated by motives of the highest love, we are doing the exact opposite.
>
> Arjuna became a coward at the sight of the mighty array against him; his "love" made him forget his duty towards his country and king. That is why Sri Krishna told him that he was a hypocrite: "Thou talkest like a wise man, but thy actions betray thee to be a coward; therefore stand up and fight!"[1]

[1]Vivekananda, S., *The Yogas and Other Works,* p. 463. New York: 1953.

Even though a person is not ready to practice it, the ideal of non-resistance of evil should always be held in sight. A person who shoots at the sky shoots higher than he who shoots at a tree. If you think your whole ethical ideal is just to practice a little virtue while always putting your own interests first, you can never attain the Supreme Goal.

If one knows that "resist not evil" is the supreme ethical principle, even if it is only intellectually understood, this will help him to rise gradually to the highest level. But he will have to reach this ideal from wherever he happens to be.

So a person should understand his own psychological condition and his situation in life. If he knows that, and if he knows the spiritual and ethical ideal, he can gradually guide his steps toward the attainment of this ideal.

My teacher used to emphasize the principle of returning good for evil when speaking to monastic disciples. He said that if you do good in this world, it often happens that those persons you help will be very critical of you. Those you do nothing for will not criticize you much, but those who receive benefit from you may always be critical.

It sometimes seems that people are so ungrateful, but we should always be prepared to do good to others though they appear that way. "Do not expect any kind of gratitude," he said. "Do your own part of serving human beings, seeing God in them, and never return evil for evil." He illustrated this teaching with a story.

One day a holy man was seated on the bank of the Ganges where he was practicing his daily meditation, worshipping the Lord. All of a sudden he noticed that a scorpion was drifting away in a current of the river. Taking pity on the scorpion, he took it in the palm of his hand and put it safely on the ground.

But after a while, he found that the scorpion had again fallen into the water, and was again being carried away by the current. A second time he took it in his palm and put it back on the ground. Each time the scorpion stung him, and he felt severe pain.

Before long, yet for the third time the holy man found the scorpion in the water, being carried away. Though he was feeling much pain from the stinging he had twice received, he again took the scorpion and put it very far from the water.

Standing not far away, an observer had been watching the holy man take the scorpion each time from the water, being stung each time, and still trying to save the scorpion. So he asked, "Sir, I noticed that you took the scorpion in the palm of your hand and were badly stung, and still you helped — three times. What is the reason?"

"You see," replied the holy man, "it is the nature of the scorpion to sting, but the nature of a holy man to always help everyone. So if the scorpion cannot give up its nature, why should I give up mine?"

From very ancient times, this principle of returning good for evil has been taught by the great spiritual teachers of the world. It is the highest ethical principle, commensurate with the great spiritual truths. This principle is based on the vision of one Supreme Spirit penetrating the whole universe, dwelling in the hearts of all as the inmost self, as the Soul of all souls.

Persons who develop this vision automatically become established in returning good for evil. It becomes part of their nature, and they have to make no effort to practice it. Others, who have not reached this culmination of spiritual life, do have to make persistent efforts.

The highest principles should always be kept in mind, however low our present moral and spiritual status may be. Then even if we cannot practice it at once, by gradual steps we can rise to the level of non-resistance.

CHAPTER VIII

The Divine Law of Karma

DIVINE law and divine grace are apparently contradictory. Law means the enforcement of justice, while grace means mercy. If God is all-just, how can He be all-merciful at the same time?

We know that justice is conditional. As you sow, so shall you reap. If you do good deeds you experience the good results; if you do evil deeds you suffer the consequences. Under law one is accorded what is due — punishment or reward.

But grace is unconditional; it does not consider your deservingness or undeservingness. Grace comes freely. You get it simply because you want it or ask for it. So how can both divine law and divine grace prevail in this world at the same time?

The answer is that each has its own province. Because they operate in two different spheres of human life, there is scope for the function of both divine law and divine grace.

It is true that divine law controls the whole universe, but divine law associated with justice prevails only in human life. There is no question of judging the actions of animals and inanimate objects. They have their own way, and function according to the natural laws of God.

You do not pass judgment if one stone falls and breaks another. Neither do you punish a tiger for devouring a lamb; that is his nature. On the subhuman level instinctive actions prevail. Trees, plants and animals are alive just as human beings are, and they may perceive and feel also, but only human beings have the capacity for self-awareness. So it is only on the human level that volitional action prevails.

There are two distinctive functions which set human life apart. First, man has freedom of judgment. He has the capacity to judge what is right or wrong, what is good or evil, what is high or low. Secondly, man can act according to these judgments; he has freedom of action. He can act one way, he can act the opposite way, or he can act neither way.

This freedom of will is a great privilege, and at the same time a great responsibility. Privilege means additional responsibility because you have to account for your actions while exercising that privilege. Because of man's privilege of freedom in judgment and action, he is held responsible for his deeds under divine law. It is this privilege of *karma* which distinguishes the human level from all other levels of life.

Karma is usually translated as work, but it has a much wider and deeper significance than the English word *work*. Generally speaking, the Sanskrit term *karma* means volitional action, though that still does not give a complete picture of what *karma* is. Any volitional use of the body, the organs, or the mind is all *karma*. Whatever you think, know, watch, imagine, or remember is all *karma* as long as it is deliberately or knowingly done.

If you sit down on a park bench to watch what is going on in the street, you are doing *karma*. Even if you lie down intentionally in order to avoid doing work, this is also *karma*. But you would not call it work. That is why if you deliberately use any of the factors in the human personality, as long as it is volitional, it is *karma*.

Besides volitional actions, there are involuntary and instinctive activities carried on in the human system. *Karma* does not include what we call autonomic and reflex actions.

You may be seated while at the same time breathing and digesting your food. Though it is your physical body that is doing all of this, the digestion, like the breathing, is involuntary and so is not included in *karma*. If something is brought very close to your eye, your eyelid will automatically close. This is a reflex action so it is not *karma* either.

Karma implies self-determination; it is *karma* that distinguishes human beings from all other creatures in the world. There is no *karma* on the subhuman level, because there all actions are either instinctive, involuntary, or reflexive. There is no self-determination. Only the conscious, deliberate activities of human beings are signified by the word *karma*.

The *karma* that we do has two effects: one is an immediate, visible effect; and the other is a remote, invisible effect. If you hurt another person you may or may not have any regret, but that person obviously suffers. If you feed a child, when its hunger is gone it is satisfied, and you may also feel satisfaction. These are the immediate effects of *karma.*

But there is also a subtle, invisible effect which finds expression later. With the performance of *karma,* you acquire impressions within you. The actual experience allied with *karma* is only temporary, but the impression left by that experience is indelible and lasting. Anything you see, anything you hear, anything you do, think, or know creates internal impressions. We are constantly gathering these impressions within us through all of our perceptions, through all of our cognitions, through all of our actions.

Out of these impressions our memories grow, our likes and dislikes develop, our disposition is created. A wrong habit creates a wrong tendency. But if a person continues a good action in order to cultivate some power, out of the impressions that are accumulated by slow practice, that power also grows. Not only our habits, but our talents and capacities develop as a result of the accumulated impressions of *karma.*

If you persistently practice a musical instrument, you develop the talent to play that instrument efficiently through the impressions that are accumulated by this practice. You may develop your capacity to write, for example, by writing a little every day. It is so with regard to each and every action we perform repeatedly; practice does make perfect.

But even if an action is performed only once, that also leaves an impression on the mind. Our likes and dislikes grow out of these impressions, which never leave us.

Agreeable and disagreeable feelings are constantly bubbling up from these impressions. That is why the mind is so restless. Even when you do not react to agreeable or disagreeable objects outside you, still these feelings are created within you.

So the impressions we gain through volitional action become the source of our memories and feelings. They build our dispositions, and also develop our talents.

Apart from that, these impressions remain within us as merits and demerits — as retributive forces. Mechanical action may produce an immediate effect, but it does not leave an impression which can fructify in the future to create a favorable or an unfavorable situation. That is, these impressions can be judged from the moral standpoint.

You can do something which is economically very good for the country, but morally it may be very bad. Whatever we do consciously and deliberately produces not only an immediate result, but also lies within us as a latent moral result. These impressions fructify in the course of time, and create favorable or unfavorable situations for us here or hereafter.

St. Paul refers to the law of *karma* and its inevitable justice in his Epistle to the Galatians (6:5,7-9):

> For every man shall bear his own burden.

> Be not deceived; God is not mocked; for whatsoever a man soweth, that shall he also reap.

> For he that soweth to his flesh shall of the flesh reap corruption, but he that soweth to the Spirit shall of the Spirit reap life everlasting.

And let us not be weary in well doing: for in due season we shall reap, if we faint not.

If we indulge in wrong deeds, in consequence of these wrong deeds we encounter an unfavorable situation here or hereafter. If we do good and virtuous deeds, we encounter a favorable situation here or hereafter. But whatever kind of deeds we do, in due time we will receive the results of those deeds.

Of course, nobody gathers only wrong impressions, and those who perform right deeds also perform some wrong deeds; so these impressions are of a mixed character.

Suppose a person by repeated effort succeeds in dominating his evil tendencies and performs mostly good deeds. As a result of this he will have some kind of well-being in life. He will have happiness, prosperity, and a better position in life. But if the impressions are on the whole bad, they will produce some kind of disagreeable situation. You might lose honor, lose money, lose a position, lose friends, suffer from some kind of incurable disease, or meet death by accident.

So these impressions, apart from creating our tendencies, talents, likes, dislikes, and memories, also serve as moral forces leading us to favorable or unfavorable situations in life. It is very important that we know what we are achieving by our conscious, deliberate actions.

The forces of these actions always lie within us. They produce certain results in this life. But still there are many of these impressions of merit or demerit that may not fructify in this very life and will be in store for the future. These impressions must produce results — "As ye sow, so shall ye reap."

Without acknowledging that there is something in man which is immortal, the law of *karma* could not function. One life is too limited for it. *Karma* acknowledges that man is not just a physical or psychophysical being, but is really the immortal Spirit within.

When a person dies, it does not mean the end of his existence. He has to carry the bundle of his *karma* with him. When we die there isn't a single thing in the physical world we can take with us, while there is nothing of the mind that we may leave behind. The mind is not separate from the departing spirit, and all of the accumulated *karmic* impressions dwelling deep in the mind go with the soul.

You leave the world with whatever talents you may have, whatever weaknesses or excellences you have acquired, whatever merits or demerits you have ac-cumulated. With only that collection of mental contents you have to depart, and it is that collection which determines your future course. If you acquire certain skills with the hands, for example in painting or playing the violin, the skills that you have developed go with you after death. The deeper your attention in your activities, the deeper the impressions left by those activities.

For better or worse, this moral force of *karma* cannot be avoided. Death cannot nullify the influence of *karma;* distance cannot avert it; time cannot erase it. Sometime or other it will fructify. It may be after one year or fifty years, after one lifetime or many, but the results of your conscious actions will come to you.

According to the doctrine of *karma,* man has to come here to earth. It is only on the human plane that one has the power to think, the power of freedom of choice and freedom of action. Because of this, human beings have the greatest possibility of moral and spiritual development.

In the subhuman plane there is no moral life. There may be creatures much more innocent than human beings, still they cannot be counted as moral beings.

As a result of man's moral choices he accumulates impressions deep within the mind, and because of these accumulated merits and demerits we are born in our situations on earth. Each and everyone is born with a particular psychophysical system; each and everyone is born in a certain environment; and each and everyone will go through certain experiences and live for a certain period of time.

Each situation in life is different in some way from all other situations. The law of *karma* is the only suitable explanation of these differences and the many other anomalies of life. Heredity does not explain them, predestination does not explain them. But the law of *karma* does. It does not make God or some unknown fate responsible for your situation in life, it makes you responsible: you are what you struggle for. Your present situation has been determined by your past actions, and your future will be determined by your present actions.

Karma does not mean that your mental and physical movements are completely fixed by your past actions, though they are determined in a general way. Past actions have created certain conditions for you, and you are working under those conditions, so naturally you have certain limitations. For example, you can carry a load on your back according to your strength, and though with the load you cannot move as freely as you can without the load, still you have a good deal of freedom of movement.

Sri Ramakrishna said man's freedom is like that of a cow tied to a post. Though the cow cannot go beyond the length of the rope, it can graze, lie down, stand up or sit down and do many other things within the reach of its tether.

In spite of the situations created for us by our past *karma,* we have a certain freedom of action, and we can modify our conditions to a great extent. Through effort we can improve our physical health, and we can improve our mental health. Though we are restricted in our freedom of choice, through careful use of that freedom we can greatly change the effect of past actions.

When it is said that the result of *karma* is inevitable, it does not mean that nothing can be done about it, that it cannot be mitigated. A person may have a physical handicap, but in spite of that he can make progress in life. He need not succumb to that handicap. Because it is your creation, you have to accept your situation in life — you need some kind of resignation to your past existance.

But at the same time you must be hopeful about your future, because it is you who have created the situation and you who have the power to change what you have done.

Although you may not be able to undo it completely, you can still modify conditions to a great extent.

Karma is inevitable because it will not die of itself if left alone. Wherever you go your impressions will go with you, and if nothing is done about them, they will dwell within you indefinitely, even beyond death. This is the meaning of inevitability.

If something is thrown from the roof of a house, it will inevitably fall to the ground if there is nothing to obstruct its passage. Similarly, karma is always waiting for the opportunity for fructification. In due course every *karmic* cause has a corresponding and appropriate effect, but man does have the ability to counteract these effects of past impressions to a great extent.

Karma is based on the recognition that man is not just an automaton. He has freedom of will, however limited that freedom may be. Whether he can use his freedom rightly or wrongly is a different question, but man does have that freedom, and through the law of *karma* that makes him responsible for his actions. You determine your situation in life, favorable or unfavorable, and in spite of your handicaps you can make progress in it.

Usually *karma* works in two distinct channels. You are born with a particular body, and with a mind containing certain latent desires and tendencies. These tendencies first lead us to certain activities, which can be counteracted by education and right association. That is the purpose of going to school, or of receiving moral and spiritual instruction.

For instance, a person may have a tendency to talk

badly about others, yet by proper instruction and the good example of those around him he may counteract this tendency.

Secondly the impressions of *karma* may lead to sufferings, or pleasures, or enjoyments. If a person has done some wrong deeds, he has stored impressions which will seek an opportunity to cause him suffering. Because of these impressions he may lose some wealth, or honor, or a loved one. He may be born with a physical disability, or contract a serious illness. Or if a person has done many good deeds he may enjoy a favorable situation in life with success and prosperity.

This type of experience which we go through because of past actions cannot be altered very much by our present activities. We cannot avoid suffering or bereavement simply by education. Still, though it is much harder to do, it is possible to mitigate even the *karma* that leads to inevitable sufferings through virtuous deeds and prayer to the Lord. However although we cannot always avoid bad experiences, the tendencies in the mind that *karma* creates toward activities can be greatly changed by education and right association.

Suppose a person is born blind. He cannot cure his blindness, for we cannot take as much liberty with the body as with the mind. But in spite of his blindness, he can completely change his attitude toward life.

A person with physical disabilities can be always fretting about them, or he may adopt a spirit of resignation and utilize his present situation with a hopeful attitude for the future. He will not suffer as much, and he can so improve his inner nature that though he is blind he will be happy and peaceful. This is the freedom a person has in spite of his limitations.

A human being has to be judged not by his physical disabilities, not by the color of his skin or the poverty in which he was born, but by the attitude with which he lives in this world. This is a great teaching of the doctrine of *karma*. *Karma* says that whatever your situation in life, you must make the best of that situation both mentally and physically, because to a great extent you have the freedom to do so.

According to the law of *karma*, there is no accidentalism, or predestination, or fatalism. It does not lay the blame for your misfortune on God or some uncertain fate. *Karma* makes you wholly responsible for your situation in life. It inevitably produces effects, but you can mitigate these effects through your own efforts and the help of others. Though we are limited in many ways by past actions, we are very much the makers of our own fate.

The whole universe is governed by the law of cause and effect, and applied to human existence this is the law of *karma*. Essential to this divine law is the fact that man has freedom of will, and it is this freedom that makes a person responsible for his conditions in life. Human beings reap the fruits of their good or bad actions under the law of *karma*, and are rewarded or punished accordingly.

But it is possible through the performance of good deeds to go beyond the results of both good and bad actions. Though *karma* binds you, *karma* itself can also lead you to complete freedom.

As long as a person holds to the ego, he is bound by the law of *karma* and will receive only justice for his actions. But when he tries to surrender this ego to God, gradually the law of *karma* recedes and the mercy of God descends upon his life. Through this surrender to the Lord one can leave the realm of divine law, and enter the realm of divine grace.

CHAPTER IX

Divine Grace

Howern good man's activities may be, they cannot take him beyond the sphere of interdependence that is this world.

If through repeated efforts a person succeeds in dominating his evil tendencies and performs mostly good deeds, according to the law of karma he will have good experiences here and hereafter. There is no question that to some extent good deeds alleviate the problems of life.

But whatever security a person may have by virtue of his good activities, as a result of these activities that person still is in bondage. Because of good actions the chain around a person's neck may change from iron to gold, but that is the only difference. Both are equally strong to bind.

Just as want binds us, prosperity also binds us. Just as lack of beauty is a bondage, so beauty is also a bondage. As long as a person is in this relative existence, he will be in chains in one form or another. Every action has a limited force, so actions cannot produce unlimited or eternal results.

We cannot go beyond this world of interdependence simply by good deeds, because even good deeds have their own limitations. Every kind action requires some misery to function, and forgiveness cannot be exercised without some wrong deed. All moral virtues have their own limitations. They are conditionally good, but not absolutely good, and cannot take man out of this relative, interdependent existence.

After experiencing what good actions can bring him, a person begins to realize the shortcomings of good deeds. He begins to see the inadequacy of power and prosperity and all the blessings that the world can bring.

We are constantly trying to eliminate evil and secure good, and we think that sometime or other we shall be able to eliminate evil completely from the world and have good and good alone. A young person starts life with this idea: "It is true that many others have a defective life, but I will make my life perfect, free from all difficulties. I shall have only happiness and freedom in my life."

But inevitably something happens, and that person does not have a life unmarred by pain or bondage. When a person realizes this inevitability of the mixture of good and evil in this life, he seeks something beyond relative existence; beyond this drama of smiles and tears, hopes and fears, loves and hates.

There is no situation in this world that is the kind of freedom the human mind really longs for. A person really wants to be free in every sense, to have life where there is no trace of death, light where there is no trace of darkness.

When a person becomes disillusioned with dualities, he knows that his real goal is not anything in this world, but far beyond it.

Man's real goal is Supreme Good — good in the absolute sense — and that means God. In Him alone is the perfection of beauty, the perfection of knowledge, the perfection of love. We live in the realm of relative good, but if we seek absolute good, where there is no trace of evil, where there is complete freedom, then we shall have to seek God and God alone. He alone is beyond relativity.

In St. Mark a well-to-do person came running to Jesus Christ and asked Him:

> Good Master, what shall I do that I may inherit eternal life? And Jesus said unto him, Why callest thou me good? there is none good but one, that is, God. (St. Mark 10:17-18)

If you wish to be perfect as the Father in Heaven is perfect, you have to reach God. You cannot fulfill your deepest longing for perfection — your desire for eternal life and freedom from all bondages — simply by doing good deeds.

One has to be convinced not only of the bitterness, suffering, and misery of this life, but also of the inadequacy of pleasure and prosperity. Only then can one seek God for God's sake, God as the Supreme Ideal, as the Supreme Goal.

Through the performance of good deeds, the mind is purified and one becomes conscious of the limitations of his own ego. Most of us ignore or deny God, and our egos are inflated to such an extent that we hold ourselves responsible not only for our own lives, but for the whole world, as if the world cannot get along without our help.

When the mind is purified through the performance of right actions and a person realizes the limitations of right actions, he also realizes the limitations of his own individual power and knowledge. At the back of all individuals there is one source of all power, one source of all knowledge, all life, all joy.

When a person realizes this, he knows that if he wants true freedom he has to seek it where there is absolute freedom. He has to seek the Supreme Being who is absolutely good. Even Jesus Christ Himself, out of His extraordinary humility, did not assert Himself as good. God alone is good in the absolute sense.

When a person becomes conscious of his own limitations and becomes aware of the Divine source, he turns his thoughts towards that source. Only there can one find real freedom, real light, real joy.

Karma produces an inevitable result in this life: good begets good, bad begets bad. Whether with an iron chain or a gold one, a person is tied down to this relative existence. A person must find a way to complete freedom, yet it is not possible to just give up *karma*.

Karma produces an effect because we do work and claim the work to be our own; we naturally claim the fruits of our labors. Such egoism prevails in human life: "I have done this; I have earned that, it is mine." When a person does work with the idea that he is the doer of the work, the results of his work come back to him, that is, *karma* reacts upon him.

It is not *karma* that actually binds one, it is the ego-idea associated with *karma.* As long as egoism prevails a person is bound under law. But when a person gives up the ego-consciousness that "I am the doer, I must have the results of this work," he enters the realm of grace, and leaves *karma* behind.

When we become disillusioned with the dualities in this life and longing for the eternal grows within us, then we seek God and surrender this ego to Him. The great spiritual teachers say that it is the ego-idea that keeps man bound, and the way to freedom is to surrender this ego to the Lord. The *Bhagavad Gita* emphasizes that we must not be ego-centered, but try to be God-centered. There is only one source for each and everything in this universe, and that source is God.

It is a wrong idea that because you exercise a small amount of power, whatever you do through that power is yours. You also claim many things to be your own. At best you are a custodian of things for the time being. You cannot keep anything as long as you like, or in the way you like. You can lose whatever you have at any time. Even this physical body you cannot control very well. It does not grow in exactly the way you want it to, or last in the way you would like. You cannot actually claim anything to be your own.

So give up this idea of ownership which comes because you claim work to be your own. Live in this world merely as an instrument, a caretaker. This is the practice of *karma yoga.* When a person gives up this ego to the Lord and works with a spirit of self-surrender, he gradually becomes freed from the trammels of *karma*.

As long as one holds to the ego he is governed by law. But when he surrenders this ego to the Supreme Lord, then he enters into the sphere of grace. He cannot be held responsible for his own actions, because wrong actions become impossible if the surrender is complete.

When one works with the right attitude and does not claim any action to be his own, the results of his actions do not effect him any more. *Karma* no longer produces impressions on his mind, and it is these impressions that bind us in the future to this relative existence. Actions react upon us because we expect a return of some kind, so the reactions come back as a result. But if you give up these returns, actions will no longer react upon you.

When a person forgoes all claim to his own actions, he does not acquire any new *karma*. At the same time, the deposits of past *karma* remaining in the mind gradually become eliminated, so that a person is not affected even by his own deeds. In this way he enters into the realm of grace.

His actions become naturally pure, and they no longer bind him to this world. He becomes detached, and does not hold youth, beauty, wealth or position to be ideals in themselves. He looks upon this relative existence, this human life, only as a stairway to reach the Supreme Ideal. By attaining grace his life is unaffected by the world.

This attainment of grace is possible for anyone who can cultivate a spirit of self-surrender and accept the Supreme Being as the sole Goal, the sole Refuge, the sole Ideal; but this requires practice. As long as a person cannot have complete self-resignation to the Lord, he will have to overcome the ego-idea with self-effort.

If you want success and prosperity in this world you have to make efforts for it, and so in spiritual life there is ample scope for self-effort. It is a wrong idea to say that "I do not have to do anything for God's grace. If I seek spiritual treasures it is God's concern, he will give them to me." Do not delude yourself this way.

God has given us freedom, though limited; so one has to utilize that freedom. Through that freedom you try to improve your material life, and by that freedom you try to gain spiritual treasures also.

God expects this much from you: that by exercising your freedom, you come to sacrifice that freedom when you realize its limitations. As Jesus Christ said, "He that loseth his life for my sake shall find it." (St. Matt. 10:39) When you forego this ego and surrender yourself to God, then Divine grace comes.

Those who perform right deeds, those who do their duties in life; those who associate with the right types of persons, read the scriptures, and perform worship of God — these persons generally develop this spirit of self-resignation.

There is no partiality in God's grace. It is ready to descend on anyone, but you must open your door to receive it. As Sri Ramakrishna said, you have to unfurl the sail of your vessel of life, then God's grace will fill the sail and you will move smoothly towards the Goal. But when ego intervenes, one cannot have the advantage of Divine grace.

Sunlight is struggling to enter your room, but you keep the curtains tightly closed. If you just remove them from the way of the sun, its light will enter. Similarly Divine grace is free and always waiting to enter our lives, but our egoism blocks the way.

Egoism means the denial of God, or ignoring Him. You forget the source and assert yourself as the owner. You assert yourself as the doer, as if this knowledge belongs to you, as if this power belongs to you. You are not actually the owner of anything, and must relate each and everything to the one source of all. If you do not do that and assert your ego, law will take care of you. But if you surrender the ego, then grace functions in your life.

Jesus Christ said, "Knock, and it shall be opened unto you." (St. Luke 11:9) Yet if God is all-merciful, why does He expect even this much, that I must knock and then the door will be opened? He could easily open the door. "Seek, and ye shall find," said Jesus Christ. Why? Because God knows our limitations, and the greatest limitation is our defiance.

We deny God and think "I am the master of my life, without God's help I can get along very well in this world." Grace cannot meet this spirit of defiance. It is too tender for that. Grace comes when there is humility; when there is submission. Otherwise it is not the proper situation for grace to function.

Everything in this world has its way. Justice has its way, and grace also has its way. As long as you hold to your ego and try to defend yourself by all kinds of defense mechanisms, you are subject to justice and law. But when you give up your egoistic defiant attitude, submit yourself to the Supreme Lord and implore His mercy, then mercy comes to you. Just as it happens in the human world, there is also in the spiritual world the province of law, and the province of mercy. But you must ask for mercy to be given, and then God will always help you.

This self-surrender should be genuine, for there may be false submission also. If we do something good and reap the good results, we think "I have done this all by myself and now I am getting the benefits I deserve." But if something goes wrong and you suffer, then you say, "Oh, God has made me suffer in this world." This kind of resignation to God will not do. Both good and evil have to be surrendered completely.

With all of our excellences and weaknesses we should submit ourselves to God, and not present to Him the excellences only. "Whether I am good or evil, whether I am wise or unwise, pure or impure, I surrender myself to Thee completely." This should be your attitude. You cannot approach God with all of your credentials. When in good faith you surrender yourself as you are to the Lord, at once His grace will descend upon you.

Sri Krishna says to Arjuna in the *Bhagavad Gita* (IX:30-31):

> Even a sinful person, if he worships Me with unswerving devotion, must be regarded as righteous, for he has formed the right resolution. He soon becomes righteous and attains eternal peace. Proclaim it boldly, O son of Kunti, that my devotees never perish.

You may say, how can a sinful person surrender himself to God? Human nature is very intricate. No human mind is absolutely bad. No human mind is absolutely good. Sometimes it may happen that a person who is generally very good may be overpowered by evil tendencies, and he will appear to us as a very wicked person, as a sinful person. But as a matter of fact his good nature is only over-powered at that time.

Similarly, we often find in this life that there are some individuals who appear to us as sinful, as wicked. But those who can look into the depths of the human mind can see that underneath these weaknesses there are strong points and excellences also. It is characteristic of the small person to judge others by their weak points. But it is the special characteristic of great personalities that they judge others by their strong points.

We find in the lives of the great saviors many persons fallen in the eyes of human beings, who have been accepted by God and rescued through the great saviors. These persons may have some very strong point, and because of that turn to God and pray for His mercy. They have developed some faith which is lacking in many righteous persons.

To all appearances a person may be very sinful, but he may have attained something within himself which we do not see. The great spiritual leaders see that. In the life of Buddha we find that the courtesan Ambapali received his grace. In the life of Jesus Christ, His grace was given to Mary Magdalene. In the life of Sri Ramakrishna also, Girish

Chandra Ghosh received his grace. Such a person, because of his inner goodness, can surrender him or herself to God and receive God's grace.

For those persons who are virtuous, there cannot be any question with regard to God's grace; they are sure to receive it. Sri Krishna says (B.G. XII:6-7):

> Persons who surrender all their actions to Me, or perform all actions as an offering to Me, regarding Me as the sole goal, knowing Me to be the sole support of the universe, and worship Me with wholehearted devotion, I rescue them from this ocean of mortality.

St. Paul also says "By grace ye are saved." (Ephesians 2:5)

The one condition for God's grace is that a person has to surrender his ego to the Supreme Lord. God gives not only spiritual treasures, He even gives material possessions and fulfills man's material needs. Sri Krishna says (B.G. IX:22):

> Persons who are so devoted to me that their whole heart and mind go unto Me without thinking of anything else, they who worship Me in all beings and meditate on Me; out of grace I guard what they have and I secure what they have not; their welfare is assured through Me.

We can expect no greater expression of God's grace than this statement.

If just a little fraction of the mind can be turned to God, that is a great blessing. But if anyone is so blessed that his whole mind goes to God and he fails to think of his own necessities of life, then God promises to provide them. Jesus

Christ said in St. Matthew (6:33): "But seek ye first the kingdom of God and his righteousness; and all these things shall be added unto you."

A person may gain material possessions, but these are not considered the true manifestation of God's grace in one's life. In the true sense His grace comes in the form of spiritual treasures, which do not rust or rot, which no one can deprive you of. Through God's grace one can have material benefits, but the real indication of His grace is spiritual illumination, inner purity, inner strengh, inner light, inner joy. And that does not come until one truly surrenders oneself to God.

St. Paul says with regard to the devotees who surrender themselves to God: "For sin shall not have dominion over you: for ye are not under the law, but under grace." (Romans 6:14)

We find that God's grace works in two ways:
A person who surrenders himself to God becomes free from all attachment to the sense world and loves everything through God, as God's possession. It is our attachment to things that compels us to do wrong deeds; when we are freed from these attachments through self-surrender, we cannot do anything wrong.

Secondly, any wrong tendencies that a person has already acquired are gradually eliminated through grace.

So in both ways, sin cannot have dominion over us when we move from the sphere of law to that of grace. Being free from attachment, a person cannot do sinful deeds, and because God's grace works upon him, his past sins are also eliminated.

There are three ways in which one is able to work in this world. One can do evil deeds, one can do good deeds, or one can work doing good deeds, giving up egoism.

Unillumined, selfish persons indulge in wrong deeds. Persons who have developed a certain understanding perform right deeds. And persons who have become disillusioned of relativity perform work striving to be free from egoism. This is the practice of *karma yoga,* the way illumined spiritual aspirants work.

Thus even in this life a person can see God and be completely free from all bondages. According to our situation in life we can take up many different forms of work, but it is only work done for spiritual benefit with self-surrender to God that can make us free forever.

The great teachers of the world have recognized both the province of law and the province of grace in human affairs. As long as a person ignores God and holds to this ego, this little self, he is under law, and justice takes care of him.

But for anyone who can cultivate a spirit of self-surrender and accept God as the sole Goal, the sole Refuge, the sole Ideal — then God's mercy at once descends in his life and he receives the supreme blessing of Divine grace.

CHAPTER X

Ye Must be Born Again

THERE was a man of the Pharisees, named Nicodemus, a ruler of the Jews:

The same came to Jesus by night, and said unto him, Rabbi, we know that thou art a teacher come from God; for no man can do these miracles that thou does, except God be with him.

Jesus answered and said unto him, Verily, verily, I say unto thee, Except a man be born again, he cannot see the kingdom of God.

Nicodemus saith unto him, How can a man be born when he is old? can he enter the second time into his mother's womb, and be born?

Jesus answered, Verily, Verily, I say unto thee, Except a man be born of water and of the Spirit, he cannot enter into the kingdom of God.

That which is born of the flesh is flesh; and that which is born of the Spirit is spirit.

Marvel not that I said unto thee, Ye must be born again.

The wind bloweth where it listeth, and thou hearest the sound thereof, but canst not tell whence it cometh, and whither it goeth; so is every one that is born of the Spirit.

(St. John 3:1-8)

When Jesus Christ said, "Ye must be born again," He did not refer to the doctrine of reincarnation. He meant that a person must be born again even while he is living, in this very life.

"Verily, verily, I say unto thee, except a man be born of water and of the Spirit, he cannot enter into the Kingdom of God."

Evidently this reference is to the Christian rite of baptism with water. Water is a universal symbol of purification. We use it for physical purification, for the purification of our clothes, utensils, houses, and many other things. But Jesus does not mean it in that way.

Here the word "water" is symbolic of something that purifies a person within, though we use the element "water" for external purification. Jesus Christ used the word in the sense of inner purification, as symbolic of purification of the mind. Unless your mind is purified, there is no real baptism. You are left where you began. Your inner self, inner spirit and inner mind must all be purified, or you cannot "enter into the kingdom of God."

You must also be born "of the spirit." Man is born with the body-idea; he thinks he is a physical being. At most, if he believes in spirit, he thinks that he has a spirit. However, the real standpoint is that a person *is* spirit, and has a body. You are not really a body possessing a spirit, you are essentially pure spirit with a body for a covering. But unfortunately, man thinks of himself as a physical or psychophysical being. As such he is subject to heat and cold, hunger and thirst, birth, growth, decay, and death. Sri Shankara says:

How can the body, being a pack of bones covered with flesh, a bag of filth, highly impure, be the self-existent *Atman*[1] the knower, which is ever distinct from it?[2]

There is an old fable about a student who once complained to his teacher about this idea of Shankara. "Just see how Shankara condemns the body!" the student said. "How strange! This body so charming, so attractive, he refers to as 'a bag of filth!'"

"Is it not really a bag of filth?" replied the teacher. "Is not filth coming out of your nose, your mouth, your ears, out of your eyes even, what to speak of your lower apertures? Filth is coming out of every pore of your body constantly. What else is it?"

Still the student would not accept the teaching. "I can't agree with this. Shankara takes too pessimistic a view of the human body."

Finally the teacher said to him, "Go out and find the most filthy thing you can find, worse than filth. Bring me something which you know to be the worst."

So the student searched here and there, for this and that, because he did not know which thing was the filthiest of

---

One of the greatest philosopher-saints of India, Sri (meaning holy or revered) Shankara had thoroughly studied the vast Vedic literature by the time he renounced the world at the age of eight. He lived in approximately the seventh century A.D., and organized a system of monastic denominations which still prevails today.

[1]*Atman* is the Spirit or Soul, and denotes both the Supreme Self and the individual soul, which according to non-dualistic Vedanta, are essentially identical.

[2]Shankaracharya, S., *Vivekachudamani,* v. 158, p. 60. Madhavananda, S., translator. Calcutta: 1921.

all. At last he found some human excreta, and decided, "I don't find anything filthier than this, it will have to do."

But when he went to pick it up with some sticks, the excreta cried out, "Don't touch me, don't touch me!"

"Why?" asked the student, much surprised.

"Yesterday I was a delicious piece of cake. Being in a physical body, I have become reduced to this repulsive mess. Now everyone shuns me. Don't touch me! I don't know what will happen to me if you touch me again!"

At this, the student's mind was changed, and he returned to his teacher to tell him he now understood.

So what is the effect of this body-idea, of our identification with our physical selves? Because of it, man becomes ridden by inordinate sense desires. He is always attached to temporal things, seeking to secure pleasures and possessions. He tries to satisfy the demands of the body and the sense organs in whatever way possible.

Sri Shankara severely condemns how foolish a person is to think of himself as a physical or psychophysical being, constantly in the grip of sense desires which cannot be satiated. Still, a person dedicates his life to their satisfaction. He devotes his wealth, his intellectual knowledge, his physical power, his mental resources all to the satisfaction of the senses, and all because he identifies himself with this body.[1]

[1]It is worthy of note that at the very beginning of his *Vivekachudamani*, v. 3, Shankara emphasizes the importance of having attained a human body:

There are three things which are rare indeed and are due to the grace of God — namely, a human birth, the longing for Liberation, and the protecting care of a perfected sage.

Then what is a human being really? You are a person who cognizes; that is your main function. The organs themselves do not cognize. You may sit here with your eyes wide open, and still you will not see. Your ears may be open, and still you will not hear. There is another factor in the human personality which must join with the organs.

That factor is mind. Even the hands, organs of action, will not function of themselves. You cannot read a book or do any good work if your mind doesn't function. So beyond this physical being, beyond these senses, organs of action and organs of perception, there is the human mind. That mind must join with your organs, and then perception and action can take place.

Though the mind must be joined with the organs, still the mind is not the perceiver, the doer. There is one basic factor which perceives and works through all the organs: it is the "I," the ego. You say "I think, I hear, I feel, I imagine. I am happy, I am unhappy." Functioning through the organs in the waking state, this ego is your apparent self.

Yet even this ego is not the center of human personality, for behind it is the principle of consciousness.

Through the "I," a person identifies himself and relates to external objects. "My name is such and such; I hold this job; I live in this city; I have this many children; I like this; I do not like that."

But the "I" is not the real man; it is constantly changing. Your appearance, your abilities, your family and residence, your tastes, and even your name, can and do change from day to day, year to year.

Behind this changeful, fickle ego there is one central principle of consciousness; ever constant. Because of this, you recognize yourself amidst all changes. "Yesterday I was happy; today I am unhappy. Before I was young; now I am old." Who says this?

Behind your happy "I," behind your unhappy "I," behind all the changing conditions of body and mind, is the one, ever-present spiritual principle. So Shankara says:

> How can the body, being a pack of bones covered with flesh, a bag of filth, highly impure, be the self-existent *Atman,* which is ever distinct from it?

It is the *Atman,* the central principle of consciousness, which is the source of all your knowledge, the source of all your power. Because of that central principle, the mind functions, the organs function, the body functions. It coordinates all the factors in the psychophysical constitution. The object of cognition is bereft of the power of cognition, of consciousness; but the one cognizing principle cognizes all the changing conditions of the body, the organs, and the mind. It is ever-present, ever-distinct from all the objects of cognition, all conditions of body and mind.

That constant, central principle of consciousness in man is self-evident. No one has to prove the existence of his own self. Through the senses he requires proof of the existence of everything else, but not of himself, because he is essentially changeless, self-luminous — the central principle of consciousness. Even a child says "I am." You may require proof of the existence of God, but never of yourself.

Behind the changeful ego is this self-luminous principle

of consciousness, which appears as the ego when identified with man's psychophysical constitution. Unfortunately, man forgets that self-existent *Atman,* and identifies himself with his body. Shankara says:

> It is the foolish man who identifies himself with the mass of skin, flesh, fat, bones, and filth, while the man of discrimination knows his own self, the only entity that there is, as distinct from the body.

> The identification with the body alone is the root which produces the misery of birth, etc. of people who are attached to the unreal; therefore, destroy thou this with utmost care.

> When this identification caused by the mind is given up there is no more chance for rebirth.[1]

Again and again the *Upanishads* have declared that the way a person goes beyond birth, growth, decay and death is by realizing the changeless Self. There is no other way.

Anything you acquire in this world is temporal; God alone is Eternal in the midst of the non-eternal. Whatever you may gain, you will undergo reincarnation until you realize God.

Jesus said, "That which is born of the flesh is flesh." As long as you identify yourself with the physical body, the "mass of skin, flesh, fat, bones, and filth," you will have no escape from the cycle of birth, death, and rebirth.

And physical rebirth means you are subject once again to pain and pleasure, hope and fear, love and hatred, good and evil, and all the other dualities that make up this worldly existence.

[1] Op. cit., v. 159, v. 164.

You cannot enter the kingdom of God beyond dual experience unless you gain consciousness of your spiritual self.

Jesus Christ said that this can be attained even while living in this body. A person can be reborn spiritually without undergoing death. This is rebirth "of the spirit," attained through purification of the mind. Real baptism is that, otherwise it is no baptism at all.

Just a sprinkling of holy water is not the real baptism. That may be the outward symbol, but the real purpose of baptism is to change yourself within. Instead of bearing the body-idea you must recognize yourself as the Spiritual entity — "I am the eternal spirit, beyond birth, growth, decay, and death; ever-free, immortal."

Every person is in the grip of the body-idea, so how can one develop spirit consciousness? The first step is moral observances: the cultivation of virtue and overcoming of vice. For proper development of any aspect of life, whether physical development, intellectual development, aesthetic development, not to speak of spiritual development — you must be established in the path of virtue.

It is virtue which maintains the soundness of mind, the one essential condition for right development. If your mind is not sound, no external resource — even scientific knowledge —can make it so. No psychologist can cure you if you constantly allow yourself to be subject to anger, jealousy, hatred, or pride. These anti-feelings toward your fellow beings are vices which must all be overcome.

Always try to cultivate fellow-feeling toward your

fellow beings. Truthfulness, sincerity, humility, charity — these virtues must all be cultivated. This is not only the way to maintain mental health, but the first step toward spiritual rebirth.

Cultivation of virtue is the one general instruction Vedanta gives everyone, whatever his position. Neither Christianity or Vedanta objects to secular pursuits. Earn money, earn fame, earn knowledge, earn whatever you want in this world. Anything temporal you are seeking you may gain, but do not deviate from the path of virtue.

This primary instruction of Vedanta is for one's own good. When you are firmly established in virtue, you will always get the best out of this world, you will always have adequacy in life, for virtue allows you to utilize your inner and outer resources fully and wisely.

Through the observance of moral principles you will come to recognize the inherent deficiency in all worldly goals. What is that deficiency?

It is that one can't get out of the experience of dualities. Wherever you are in this world, in a mansion or a shack, with pleasure there will always be pain; with success there will always be failure; with growth there will always be decay. You will realize that secular pursuits cannot lead us beyond the dualities of good and evil. They are always present.

You may be charitable to everyone, but to whom will you be charitable unless there is misery? To whom will you be just unless there is wrong-doing? Virtue and vice go together — always. As long as we are ridden by this physical consciousness, this body-idea, we are bound to live in the world of dualities. When a person recognizes the limitations of this world, of all secular pursuits, he turns to something beyond.

There is within every individual an inherent longing for eternal life, for complete peace and blessedness, for freedom from all sorrows, from all decay, from all failure. Through the practice of virtue, a person becomes aware of this longing, and turns to the spiritual path.

It is not frustration, failure, or fear of the battle of life that turns a person toward the spiritual life. It is inner purification. As the mind is purified by moral observance, disillusionment with dualities awakens one's inherent longing for the Eternal.

As you turn to the spiritual path, you should practice *karma yoga* — the yoga of work, at the outset. That is, you should try to live in this world as a custodian only, as an instrument of the Lord. You must fulfill your obligations, but accept none of the fruits of your actions to be your own. Know everything to be His, and work in this world as a caretaker.

By doing your duties with this attitude, further purification of the mind will take place, and gradually you will recognize the limitations of the body-idea. Your mind will become purified enough to grasp the real Self, which is beyond the body, beyond the organs, beyond the mind, beyond the ego. This is the development of spiritual consciousness.

Still, it is just a primary stage. With awareness of the

spirit, you try to cultivate your spiritual knowledge. By prayer, by worship of any kind, by association with holy persons, by reading scriptures and other practices, your spiritual consciousness will be further developed, and in the course of time you will realize God.

A person who realizes God by recognizing his spiritual self, also recognizes his relationship with the Supreme Being. As Jesus Christ said, "that which is born of the Spirit is spirit." That Supreme Spirit, all-pervading, is manifest within every individual as the inmost self, inmost spirit. It is manifest as the finite center of consciousness, which is not actually separate from the infinite, all-pervading Consciousness. Gaining this, a person is spiritually reborn; because of this, there is no rebirth.

If you succeed in realizing God in this life, you will not be physically reborn. But if you die without being born of the Spirit, you will again be subject to birth, growth, decay and death. By the full development of spiritual consciousness, by realizing God, one goes beyond reincarnation.

Again and again the *Bhagavad Gita* and the *Upanishads* have said that the only way to attain immortality, to go beyond this drama of dualities, is to realize God. The *Bhagavad Gita* says (VIII:14-15):

> I am easily attainable by that steadfast spiritual aspirant who remembers me constantly and daily, with a single mind.

> Reaching the highest perfection and having attained to me, the great souled ones are no more subject to physical rebirth, which is the home of pain, and ephemeral.

Jesus Christ said "Ye must be born again." He meant man must have a second birth, a spiritual birth, even while living in this body. This rebirth must be gained through inner purification, beginning with the observance of moral principles.

When man no longer identifies himself with his physical body, he turns from the temporal realm to that of the Eternal. Through this rebirth one is born on the spiritual plane. By persistent efforts he realizes the spiritual self, recognizes his relationship with the Divinity, and ultimately succeeds in realizing God.

Through that realization one goes beyond birth, growth, decay and death. Being ever-free, he is not reborn, and lives in perpetual blessedness in the Kingdom of God.

CHAPTER XI

Worshipping God in Spirit and in Truth

"GOD is a Spirit: and they who worship Him must worship Him in spirit and in truth." Jesus Christ said this to a woman he met at Jacob's well in Samaria, while journeying back to Galilee from Judea. The passage is found in the Gospel of St. John (4:19-24):

> The woman saith unto him, Sir, I perceive that thou art a prophet.
>
> Our fathers worshipped in this mountain; and ye say, that in Jerusalem is the place where men ought to worship.
>
> Jesus saith unto her, Woman, believe me, the hour cometh, when ye shall neither in this mountain, nor yet at Jerusalem, worship the Father.
>
> Ye worship ye know not what: we know what we worship: for salvation is of the Jews.
>
> But the hour cometh, and now is, when the true worshippers shall worship the Father in spirit and in truth: for the Father seeketh such to worship him.
>
> God is a Spirit: and they that worship him must worship him in spirit and in truth.

Jesus clearly says that God is Spirit. Therefore God cannot be confined to a particular place, a particular object, or a particular name: as Spirit He is omnipresent. But though God is omnipresent, in the human stage of spiritual development, we can only worship Him through some place, object, name, or form.

It is true that God cannot be confined to Jerusalem, or Mecca, or Benaras. He cannot be identified with any particular object such as a mountain, a tree, or water, or fire. He cannot be identified with the name of Allah, or God, or Brahman. And He cannot be identified with a picture of Jesus Christ, or a statue of Buddha.

Yet the human mind has to worship Him through something concrete. If you say "God is omnipresent, so I need not think of Him in any particular way," you will feel God's presence nowhere. Most of us, truly speaking, are in this situation.

If you start with the idea that God is everywhere, so "why should I locate Him here or there," you will never be able to find God anywhere. You have to proceed in the line of least resistance, because the human mind is so constituted. In order to worship God, at least in one place in the world a person will have to feel God's presence.

If there is anything at all that gives you the feeling of God's presence, then start with that. If the sky gives you the feeling that God is there, the ruler of Heaven, think of His presence there. If there is any particular place where you feel God's presence, for example in your church, temple, or mosque, think of God as being there. If any particular image, a picture of Jesus Christ or any other image, invokes religious feelings within you, then start with that.

Let a person first feel God's presence intensely somewhere in this world. This is the beginning of worship.

Once you have that feeling of God's presence, you must remember that God is not to be identified solely with the form you have chosen. He is not to be confined solely within the place you worship Him.

"Because I worship God through fire, it is the only symbol that can signify the presence of God."

"Because I have chosen this place for worship, it is the only place where God can be worshipped."

"Because I call God by this name, it is the only name that can save human beings."

These are the mistakes we make. Though we have to worship God through a particular name, place, or form, we should remember that God is not confined in any place, in any name, in any form.

We find in the life of Sri Ramakrishna that when he went to Calcutta the carriage would pass many different places of worship. As it approached a Hindu temple, he would bow his head. Nearing a Christian church, his head would also bow. And as he passed a mosque, his head would bow yet again.

Why? Because though he was a Hindu, he knew that the very God he worshipped was also being worshipped by the Muslims in their mosque, and by the Christians in their church. That is the spirit we should maintain within us.

There is nothing wrong in worshipping God in a

temple, through a statue of Buddha, or in the name of Jesus Christ. One has to adopt a certain method. But know at the same time that your method is not the only method, your symbol is not the only symbol, and the name by which you pray to God not the only name. This is the one thing to be remembered.

If a person continues to worship the Lord in his chosen way, gradually he goes beyond form. When he learns to feel the presence of God in one particular place, his inner eye will open, and he gradually learns to feel the presence of God in other places.

As this inner eye opens, one realizes what Spirit is. Spirit is something unlike material existence, which is blind, inert, and bereft of consciousness. (That is why we call it "matter.") Spirit is completely contrary to matter. It is self-shining, of the nature of consciousness.

Because Spirit is self-luminous, you know that you are. Each and every individual, whether a child or a primitive person, knows "I am" — that he is a conscious being. Why? Because the Spirit within is self-shining.

No one has to go and prove to the child of his existence; that he sees, that he hears, that he knows. This self-awareness needs no verification from anyone. Spirit stands by its own authority, by its own right.

Behind your waking experience, behind your dream experience, behind your sleep experience, is your real Self, ever-shining pure Consciousness. This Self is behind your denial, behind your assertion. You cannot prove anything, you cannot disprove anything unless you recognize that "I am a conscious being."

If this knowledge of self-awareness is not accepted as one's very basis, you cannot do anything in this world. Whether you exercise it rightly or wrongly is a different matter, but you do have the power — self-cognition is the one central truth of our lives.

"I am" is the only direct knowledge man has; every other kind of knowledge is indirect. You may say "I see this book directly," but before "you" see anything you know the "I" that sees, you directly perceive the Self.

A physiologist would say we see when a picture-image falls on the retina, and travels the optic nerve to the brain. But where is the direct knowledge of the book?

If you perceive anything at all, it is an external sensation. Direct knowledge comes from within. Immediacy of cognition can be claimed only with regard to this Spiritual Self, ever-shining, the direct manifestation of the Supreme Spirit.

Spirit means self-effulgent Reality. Just as light in this physical world is self-shining, and illumines all objects before us while at the same time manifesting itself, similarly this light of Consciousness is manifesting the external objects, manifesting the mental states, while at the same time shining in its own glory.

When a person develops inner self-understanding, he perceives that "Yes, the principle of Consciousness that illuminates my outside world is also the one light that manifests the entire universe. It is ever-shining within my heart."

We do not find that light of pure Spirit anywhere else in the world. It shines only in living individuals. Sentiency and consciousness can be found nowhere else.

Blind nature is powerful, no doubt, but it is no power compared to the potency of the light of Consciousness. Who would submit to becoming a mighty force of nature at the cost of his self-awareness?

Pure Consciousness, the eye of the eye, the ear of the ear, the mind of the mind, the life of life — is the direct manifestation of the Supreme Spirit, the self-effulgent omnipresent Supreme Being.

When a person realizes this, he meditates on God within. "At the back of this little consciousness is the supreme, effulgent ocean of Consciousness. That Consciousness, that pure omnipresent Spirit, is shining within me, enabling me to live, to know, to think, to observe the shining Spirit." At the back of each and every wave there is one boundless mass of water we call ocean. So at the back of each and every individual consciousness, there is the universal Consciousness. Thus one meditates on God within.

For every kind of experience, there is a particular instrument. The fragrance of a flower is left untouched by the eyes, but no other instrument can perceive its color; fragrance must be left to the nose. In this way the five sense organs cannot exhaust the universe. The eyes receive the physical forms, the ears receive the physical sounds, and so with smell, touch, and taste. Only spirit receives Spirit.

When true self-understanding develops, the haze

surrounding the Self is removed, and one's inner light contacts the Supreme Spirit. The mind receives mental ideas; spirit communicates with Spirit.

As a person meditates and becomes aware of the true nature of his self, he realizes he is not just a psychophysical being, but is essentially self-shining Spirit — immortal, ageless, changeless. He finds that this individual consciousness is actually just a mode of the universal Consciousness, and he meditates on God as the Soul of his soul. Then worship of God in Spirit truly begins.

As a person continues spiritual practice, one comes to realize the deepest unity with the Supreme Being. Ultimately one perceives the Supreme Self, omnipresent, enfolding everything, shining through everything; one Being — God.

If you do not directly perceive God, the next best method is to meditate on Him. For instance, I can think of you when I am away from you, but that does not mean I am seeing you. Meditation and actual experience are two different things. When you do not actually experience or see God, you can meditate on Him. This is much better than not thinking of Him at all.

To be with you and see you is very good; but to meditate on you and think of you is the next best thing one can do. So this is the next best thing we can do for the Lord. Remember God, and meditate on Him as the effulgent Reality, pure Spirit, omnipresent.

But this is not always possible either, because meditation on God requires full concentration of the mind. Intensification of your thoughts and feelings is needed for meditation. When you cannot meditate you can pray to God, sing devotional songs, chant hymns. These things are not as difficult as meditation. Oral practice is less difficult than mental practice.

If that also is impossible for you, the next best thing is to worship God by physical methods, through material objects. Offer Him food, flowers, candles, or something you like in His name. Bow down to Him, serve His cause in as many ways as you can. Make pilgrimages, observe religious holidays and ceremonies. These physical methods are not as difficult to follow as the oral or mental methods, but through them one can gradually progress to feeling the presence of the Lord everywhere.

It is said in the *Bhagavatam* that a devotee who perceives the existence of God only in a particular place, in a particular form, or object, is on the lowest rung of the spiritual ladder. One may be a worshipper of the Lord, but if one feels that God is confined to a particular type of architecture, to this place or that place, to this picture or that statue, by this name or that name, he is just at the beginning of spiritual life.

As a person advances he feels God's presence within instead of without, ever-shining inside himself as pure Spirit. He feels that he carries God within him wherever he goes. His temple is in the innermost shrine of his heart.

At the same time one feels God's presence in all, particularly in the hearts of other devotees. Instead of finding God in a temple or an image, he feels God's presence within himself and in the hearts of other worshippers of the

Lord. This is the second stage of development.

Eventually a person finds that God is not confined within this heart or many hearts, but is the all-pervading Spirit, the omnipresent Being. It is His light that manifests and sustains this universe — He is the Light of all lights.

He shining, the sun shines; He shining, the mind shines; He shining, the moon shines, the stars gleam, the lightning flashes. He shining, everything shines. It is said in the *Upanishads,* "The highest worship is to feel the presence of Brahman, the omnipresent Being, constantly shining."

Manifested through all existence is one effulgent ocean of Light which penetrates everything. Always living in complete awareness of that Supreme, self-effulgent Reality, one performs worship of the highest order. This is worshipping God in spirit in the true sense.

Jesus Christ gave two distinct ideas for the true worshipper of the Lord — worshipping God "in spirit," and "in truth." Worshipping God in spirit has particular reference to God's nature, but what does Jesus Christ mean by worshipping God "in truth?"

It apparently refers to the worshipper's inner attitude. Worshipping God in truth, not in falsehood, is worshipping with full faith, or with as much faith and devotion as you can command. You should worship God sincerely, in spite of all your limitations and drawbacks.

The one test of sincerity is that you worship God for His sake alone. To worship God for some kind of personal gain, some transitory possession or pleasure here or hereafter, is not worshipping God with sincerity. To pray to God for help in the time of distress, and then to forget Him when the calamity passes away is not sincere worship either. One should worship God because He is the one source of all love, all joy, all freedom, all wisdom, all beauty, all strength.

If you really understand this, you can never worship Him for anything. You should worship and respect everything else, for Him. In Him is complete self-fulfillment, so why should you care for anything else? There is nothing higher than God. If you care for anything else, you should care for His sake, for the sake of reaching Him. You should not worship God for the sake of anything lower than He.

It is said that a thief once lived close to a room where there was a great treasure. But guards were always stationed there, and the thief could not find any opportunity to enter the room. How restless he was! How anxious he was to enter the room and steal the treasure!

Then one night he noticed that the guards had fallen asleep. How much more restless he became! Now he *had* to make an attempt to get the treasure.

Similarly, if you feel there is one source of all joy, of all love, of all beauty, of all strength — if you really believe this, how can you afford to sit idle and make no effort to reach it?

We say "God is the highest, He is all-merciful, He can be reached." But at the same time we cannot spare fifteen minutes a day for His sake. That does not show that we are sincere.

God has to be worshipped with sincerity. We should recognize Him as the highest and the best. We should also recognize our own shortcomings and see how we can make the most of our situation in life. There can be self-deception in faith, like anything else.

We may say "I believe in God," but actually have no faith at all. One should make sincere efforts according to one's limitations, that's all. If a person sincerely utilizes his situation for the worship of the Lord, it can be said he is worshipping God in truth.

The following story, told by Sri Ramakrishna, is about the value of such sincere belief.

Once there was a great scholar who spent much time reading the scriptures, and could quote many verses from them by memory. He was one of those persons who study religions and investigate into the nature of God for intellectual satisfaction.

Now there was a milkmaid who used to supply milk to the pundit's house, for he had children to feed. But the milkmaid was very irregular in delivering the milk, often arriving quite late. So one day the pundit scolded her and asked her why she was so irregular, causing the children to suffer.

"You should come in the early morning and not be so late."

"What can I do?" she replied, "I have to cross a river on the way, and the ferryman is sometimes late. I don't always see the ferryboat ready at the bank, so what can I do"

"What do you mean?" said the pundit, "In the name of the Lord people cross the ocean that is this world. Can you not cross that river is His name?"

The unsophisticated mind of the milkmaid took the pundit's words literally. She thought, "Yes, it is true that human beings can cross the ocean of life with the name of the Lord. Why should I not be able to cross the river in His name?"

Later, the pundit noticed that the milkmaid was bringing the milk exactly at the same hour every day. So one day he met her to find out why.

"Well, formerly you were often late. How is it you come so regularly now?"

"You told me that in the name of the Lord one can cross the river," said the milkmaid.

"You mean you don't come by the ferryboat?"

"No," replied the milkmaid, "I just walk over the water."

"Really?" The pundit was astonished. "I must see that." So he followed the milkmaid to the river and watched in amazement as she walked over the water.

"Come on, come on," she said, urging the pundit to follow.

At first he did not dare to walk into the water. However, he began to think, "All right, if she can do it, I can do it too." But as he followed the milkmaid, he pulled his clothes up around him.

Noticing this, the milkmaid said, "Why do you pull your clothes up, Sir? Have you no faith in the name of the Lord?"

This is what happens. We talk about God, we talk about faith in God and we think we have faith, but in actual practice we don't. Jesus Christ says you should worship God with all sincerity, with as much faith as you can command, with as much devotion as you can command, and see that there is no self-deception. Such a good start undoubtedly means progress towards the Supreme Goal.

If a person worships God with sincerity, accepting Him as the very Goal and knowing that this is the real mission of life, he naturally utilizes everything else for that Supreme purpose. This means he lives the way to God — he develops a basic inner attitude.

The worship of God is not fruitful until you develop such an attitude, an attitude of devotion. As long as you live in the realm of forms and objects, you may meditate for hours, say prayers, or go regularly to church. But if there is not true devotion in your heart, if you do not accept God as the true goal of life and have that transformation of your inner nature, all your religious life is simply mental and physical exertion.

Some persons say, "Well, my friend, religion is a private affair." What does that mean — "private affair?"

Does it mean that religion is just a cloak you put on for the time being to enter church and become religious, and then when you leave, it is left behind? If devotion is a basic attitude of your life, how can you leave it behind?

Real religion is not such a "thing." If it is your basic attitude, it will include your public life as well as your private life.

Sri Krishna says to Arjuna in the *Bhagavad Gita* (IX:27):

Whatever thou doest, whatever thou eatest, whatever thou offerest in sacrifice, whatever thou givest away, whatever austerity thou practicest, O son of Kunti, do that as an offering unto Me.

There is a strikingly similar verse in I Corinthians (10:31):

Whether therefore ye eat, or drink, or whatsoever ye do, do all to the glory of God.[1]

You must carry your religion through all of your activities: at home, at work, in your eating, in your drinking, in your sleeping, in your talking. If you can, it will be a real, guiding force — the potent regulating principle of your life. Then you are worshipping God in truth.

In the beginning, your devotion may be a kind of intellectual process. "Yes, there is a God and one must reach Him, otherwise there is no security anywhere." But from that calculation you have to come to the natural inflow of devotion toward God.

This natural devotion grows within a person as he continues his spiritual disciplines and maintains the right attitude. As you proceed in this way, your mind becomes more and more purified, and you will develop real longing for God.

An illustration is often given of a magnet and a piece of iron. If the piece of iron is covered with too much dirt, the magnet cannot attract it; the iron does not feel the pull of the magnet. Similarly, as long as our minds are covered with all

[1]Also Col. 3:17,23.

kinds of contrary thoughts and ideas, we do not feel the Divine attraction.

But when this dross and dirt is removed by mental, verbal, or physical forms of worship, we feel a deep longing for God. Just as we feel intense yearning for wealth, or beauty, or companionship, we can feel an intense yearning for God.

From intellectual belief, you must progress to spontaneous love. When you worship God with that kind of deep longing, you have developed much further in the worship of God in truth.

As our inner vision is clarified, we gradually perceive the truth in spiritual life. The truth is that "I am God's. I belong to Him alone." You may sell yourself to the world, or to this person or that person, but all such sales are false. You really belong to Him — everyone belongs to Him, the Supreme Master; we are all His.

So our fundamental duty in life is to pay homage to Him, recognize Him as the Supreme Master, and try to be one with Him. This is the central truth of religious life.

If you want to worship God in truth, you should feel that He alone is your eternal Father, eternal Mother, eternal Friend, eternal Companion; eternal Guide, eternal Refuge, eternal Home. He is your All-in-All. Where else is there anything that is dependable? Where else shall you seek refuge in this world?

We are seeking security in the insecure all of our lives. But now you find God to be your eternal Companion, and you realize that every other relationship is only temporary.

God alone is Eternal in the midst of the non-eternal.

You do not have to ignore or neglect anything, but utilize everything for the sake of worshipping the Lord. Everything else in life should subserve this main objective.

> In this world, O Lord, in search of wealth, I have found Thee the greatest treasure; in this world, O Lord, in search of a friend, I have found Thee the most dependable One; in this world, O Lord, in search of someone to love, I have found Thee the most lovable One.

> At Thy feet is the culmination of all knowledge; at Thy feet is the fulfillment of all desires; at Thy feet is the consummation of all love. Where else but at Thy blessed feet shall I seek refuge?

> Thou art my Mother, Thou art my Father, Thou art my friend, Thou art my Companion; Thou art my knowledge, Thou art my treasure, Thou art my All-in-All. Thou art the Soul of my soul.

When you develop this attitude of self-surrender, instead of offering only a flower or a prayer, you will offer yourself completely at the feet of the Lord. When you reach this stage, in all sincerity you will be worshipping God in truth.

CHAPTER XII

Ye Shall Know the Truth

I N the Gospel of St. John we find: "And ye shall know the truth, and the truth shall make you free." This passage can be interpreted in many different ways. We will first try to understand it with reference to the context in which it was spoken.

Then said Jesus to those Jews which believed on him, If ye continue in my word, then are ye my disciples indeed;

And ye shall know the truth, and the truth shall make you free.

They answered him, We be Abraham's seed, and were never in bondage to any man: how sayest thou, Ye shall be made free?

Jesus answered them, Verily, verily, I say unto you, Whosoever committeth sin is the servant of sin.

And the servant abideth not in the house for ever: but the Son abideth ever.

If the Son therefore shall make you free, ye shall be free indeed.   (St. John 8:31-36)

"And ye shall know the truth, and the truth shall make you free." The word *truth* has many different meanings. But how does Jesus Christ use the word truth? From the context above, it appears that He meant truth about Himself.

Being free means freedom from sins. If you know the truth about Jesus Christ — that He is the Son of God, who has been incarnated in this world for the redemption of mankind through remission of their sins — if you understand this truth, you will be free from sin. All your sins will be forgiven, and you can no longer commit sin.

But for that person who believes that Jesus Christ will take care of all of his sins, and so indulges in any amount of sin, that belief is wrong. It is a false belief. The person who truly believes that Jesus Christ is the Redeemer of mankind, that all sins are forgiven through His great mercy and compassion — that person will not commit any more sins.

If you believe Jesus Christ to be the Son of God, you will naturally follow His teachings.

Then spake Jesus again unto them, saying I am the light of the world: he that followeth me shall not walk in darkness, but shall have the light of life. (St. John 8:12)

By following His teachings you are sure to see the light of truth. You will attain life, that is, Eternal Life. Through faith in Jesus Christ and His teachings, a person will be freed not only from a sinful life, but also from all ignorance, which is the root cause of all sufferings.

Because of ignorance man is born again and again into this world; because of ignorance man undergoes all manner of hardship in this relative existence. By knowing Jesus

Christ to be the Incarnation of God and following His teachings, you can become completely free from all bondages.

A similar idea is expressed in the *Bhagavad Gita,* where Sri Krishna tells Arjuna (IV:9):

> He who thus knows, in the true light, My birth as something which is different from the birth of ordinary mortals, who knows the secret, the real significance of My birth as an Incarnation of God, and who also knows the meaning of My mission in life, he, after giving up this physical body, will attain to Me, O Arjuna, and is not born again.

That is, such a person enters into Eternal Life, through real understanding of the Incarnation of God.

Another meaning to this passage is that he who believes in God's Incarnation also believes in His infinite compassion. When you believe in the compassion of God, your heart and mind cannot but be filled with devotion to Him. It is through the Incarnation of God that we find the greatest evidence of God's compassion for humanity.

Is there any real evidence in the world of God's mercy and love for human beings? He has created many beautiful things in this world, but He has also created all manner of bad and ugly things. If God actually becomes incarnate in human flesh in order to lead human beings to complete freedom, then this is the real proof of God's compassion.

Any person who believes in the Incarnation of God must have devotion to Him. Love for God doesn't depend simply on faith in God. It also has very much to do with what kind of God we believe in. Science can give us a God, but it cannot give us devotion to Him.

Suppose you conceive of God as an omnipotent, all-knowing Being who rules over the world according to strict laws and regulations; a very stern, just Ruler. What kind of affection can you have for this Lord? You can bow down to Him at a distance, or try to propitiate Him by all sorts of prayers and offerings, but you will not be attracted to Him. You will not feel Him to be your Father, your Mother, your Friend, or your Guide.

You can have real devotion, real love for God, only when you know that He feels for you, that He is really anxious to save you from all sufferings. In order to love God you should believe in His real love for you. Real love evokes real love.

How can you know that God loves you? Through His Incarnations. Sri Ramakrishna once said that we have no idea what sacrifice God makes when He assumes a body. It is extremely painful for the Infinite to be shut up in a small, limited physical form. When you know that God Himself comes to this earth and plays the role of an ordinary human being, undergoing humiliation and persecution in order to teach you the path of liberation, to demonstrate to you the eternal spiritual principles — then you say, "Yes, there really is someone who feels for human beings, who is anxious to liberate us." Your heart becomes filled with love for God.

The *Bhagavatam* teaches that a person who meditates every morning and evening on the actions and achievements of an Incarnation of God gradually develops love for Him, and through that love becomes free. It is love that enables us to reach God and be united with Him.

We find the greatest development of spiritual devotion in those religions which believe in the Incarnation of God.

This passage also means that when you believe that the birth and actions of an Incarnation of God are transcendental, at once you understand the nature of the Supreme Spirit. The Supreme Spirit which pervades everything is ever unattached to matter; it is always pure in every way. God is everywhere, He permeates everything. Still He is beyond everything.

Jesus Christ said "Ye are from beneath; I am from above: ye are of this world; I am not of this world." Though God incarnates Himself in human form, He is not bound by the limitations of that human form. He is beyond form. He retains full divine knowledge, divine love, divine power.

A person who understands this truth will not only have devotion to God, but will also have a true understanding of the nature of God and His spiritual Reality. That spiritual Reality is something which transcends all the attributes of material existence. God is in everything, yet He is beyond everything.

A person who understands the nature of the Supreme Spirit can also understand the nature of his own spiritual self. Just as God, the Supreme Spirit, can dwell in a physical body, similarly ordinary mortals are also spirit living in physical bodies.

If you can believe in the spiritual nature of an Incarnation of God, you can believe in your own spiritual nature. You will know that you are not actually the physical body. You are actually spirit living in this physical body. You will be aware of your spiritual self, and know that just as God retains complete freedom though incarnate in human form, so each person as essentially pure spirit also retains complete freedom.

Though you appear to be subject to birth and death, growth and decay, pain and pleasure — you are really beyond all this. Your spiritual nature is always intact, and only through ignorance do you think you are born, suffer, and die.

A person becomes convinced of his spiritual nature when he understands the secret of the Incarnation of God. That knowledge alone makes him free.

"Ye shall know the truth, and the truth shall make you free" can also be interpreted in a general sense. Truth means reality, and is not necessarily truth about the Incarnation of God.

If we understand truth in a very general sense, it can mean the ultimate Reality, the Supreme Truth. When you know the Supreme Truth, you become free in every sense. There is no other way to complete freedom.

You can be partially free in many different ways. If you want to be free from want, you acquire wealth. If you want to be free from disease, you secure proper medical help. And if you want to be free from sin, you follow the path of virtue. In this way, you can have relative freedom.

But if you want complete freedom forever from all bondages and suffering, you must know the Truth. Truth alone is freedom. Ultimate Reality means that which is unconditioned, which is not dependent on anything. If you know the Supreme Reality, then you can become free in the true sense. There is no other way.

How can you know the Truth? One must have longing for it.

How can one have this craving, this desire, for Truth? Through purity of mind. "Blessed are the pure in heart for they shall see God." (St. Matt. 5:8)

In order to be pure in heart, one should refrain from wrong deeds, do one's duties in life, and practice virtue. In this way a person gradually becomes pure, acquires virtues, and is free from all vices. Then his yearning for Truth, for God, develops.

He is no longer fascinated by sense objects which cannot account for themselves. They are not the Truth. Truth means *the* Reality.

What, for example, is the real nature of a chair? A chair is just a form; there is no Truth in that of itself. If the chair were made out of a tree, you could break down the wood, analyze it chemically, and find certain elements. But even in this way the real nature of the chair, or whatever else you wish to examine, could never be found.

The chair only apparently exists of itself, because Truth is its real essence, the inner Reality in all things.

When a person develops purity of mind, yearning for real Truth comes. He can no longer be satisfied with this apparent existence. We are content with things as they appear because we do not see the true Reality which underlies all. We see things as if they existed independently in their own right; everything seems to be real unto itself.

But when our eyes are opened, we see the falsity of apparent existence. We find no reality in the form of the chair, none in the tree, and none in the wood itself —but somewhere else.

Until your mind is purified you will be satisfied with this apparent existence, and will not see the Reality behind it. Yearning for Truth, *the* Reality, comes only through purification of the mind.

When that yearning comes, what should you do? You should seek a teacher, and learn the method of spiritual practice that is best for you. Truth does not come simply through yearning. One must practice a spiritual method diligently.

Even when you see the falsity of apparent existence you cannot discard it, because your mind has become so habituated to dealing with things as they appear. Again and again you consider them to be real. And again and again you try to turn your mind toward the Supreme Reality. But even when your mind is purified to a great extent, and you have some yearning for Reality, you find you still cannot turn your heart away from this apparent existence. So you will have to make a persistent, constant effort to turn your thoughts toward the Supreme Reality.

When you struggle in this way, gradually the old tendencies to revert to apparent existence die out, and there is a natural flowing of the mind toward the Supreme Reality. Once you develop the sense that the Supreme

Reality is the ultimate abode of Truth, and dedicate your life to seeking that, then you are truly a spiritual aspirant.

There are some persons who try to grasp the Supreme Reality intellectually. They do not consider ultimate Truth to be the Supreme Goal of their lives.

For example, a research student of religion may study day and night, make many comparisons with religious facts, and spend more time and energy than a spiritual aspirant does in spiritual practice. Yet he cannot be called a spiritual aspirant because he does not look upon God, or Ultimate Truth, as the very goal of life. His mind sees things objectively, but his heart is set on other things — learning, fame, or glory. You become a spiritual aspirant only when your heart yearns for the Supreme Reality as the Ultimate Goal.

Once you feel this desire, you follow spiritual methods earnestly. After long practice, by constantly thinking and meditating on that Reality, you gradually develop an inner consciousness which perceives the Truth. Your mind becomes quiet, illumined, and you realize God.

So a person can gain freedom — complete freedom — by knowing the Ultimate Truth. It is the truth about the Supreme Reality, God.

To attain this knowledge, one should first purify himself by right deeds and moral actions. When this purification comes, a person will understand the vanity of this apparent, worldly existence. By practicing meditation, worshipping the Lord in all possible ways, and offering all deeds to Him, gradually one's thoughts will turn from the temporal to the Eternal, from the finite self to the Self of all.

Truth cannot be realized objectively as something outside yourself. "He who knows Truth, becomes Truth." By knowing perfect Truth, which is the Self of All, you yourself become perfect — ever-free from all bondages, all ignorance. "Ye shall know the truth, and the truth shall make you free."

CHAPTER XIII

Crucifixion and Death

IN one sense, Good Friday is one of the darkest days in human history. For on this day Jesus Christ, who came to save mankind from death, was crucified. But He was not really killed. He arose from the dead the following Sunday, demonstrating to the world that there is no death for the real man. Death may fall on this physical body, but the real Self of man, the spiritual man, is immortal.

Man thinks of himself as dying simply because he identifies himself with the physical body. St. Paul says in his Epistle to the Romans (8:6): "For to be carnally minded is death; but to be spiritually minded is life and peace." Through His crucifixion and resurrection Jesus Christ shows humanity the way to go beyond birth and death to everlasting life.

In order to understand the resurrection of Jesus Christ, we should first understand the significance of His crucifixion. The two are very closely allied, forming a single event which is the heart of the Christian religion.

Though the most stress is always given to the resurrection, the crucifixion is no less important. Crucifixion, it is said, proves the love of Jesus Christ for humanity, while resurrection proves His divinity. It would seem that crucifixion proves His divinity as well, for it is the full demonstration of what Jesus Christ stood for.

Through His crucifixion, Jesus sets before us the path we can follow to realize immortality. He gives us a model, a complete example of His teachings, that we might follow that model according to our capacities and conditions in life. It is by being His followers through crucifixion that we can attain what He attained. Through crucifixion we too can attain resurrection.

Jesus Christ accepted crucifixion of His own accord, although He easily could have prevented it. Jesus says in St. John (10:17-18):

> Therefore doth my Father love me, because I lay down my life, that I might take it again.

> No man taketh it from me, but I lay it down of myself. I have power to lay it down, and I have power to take it again. This commandment have I received of my Father.

When the multitude came to take Him, by miraculous powers Jesus could have punished them and saved Himself. But He did not. When Simon Peter drew his sword and cut off the ear of a servant of the high priest, Jesus said, "Put up thy sword into his place: for all they that take the sword shall perish with the sword." (St. Matt. 26:52) Jesus then healed the man's ear, and delivered Himself into the hands of the multitude. He willingly allowed Himself to be crucified, while forgiving those who did it.

This example of non-resistance He sets before us all. It is not a passive teaching, but the active returning of good for evil.

> Love your enemies, bless them that curse you, do good to them that hate you, and pray for them which despitefully use you, and persecute you. (St. Matt. 5:44)

Jesus Christ demonstrated the very perfection of this teaching in His own crucifixion. When He was on the cross, He prayed to the Divine Lord, "Father, forgive them; for they know not what they do." The cross is our symbol of the compassion, forgiveness, and universal love that Christ gave us by allowing Himself to be crucified.

Non-resistance of evil is the highest principle of spiritual life, and one cannot truly exemplify this teaching unless he is established in the Oneness of the spiritual Self. The cross, symbol of His crucifixion, proves how Jesus overcame the flesh by a consciousness of the Spirit. It is this conquest of the flesh that brings immortality.

We have to overcome our lower selves by our higher Selves. The fulfillment of life is not in physical development; it is not in intellectual development, nor even in moral development. It is in spiritual development. That alone can make you strong, can make you free, can give you love.

You attain that by consciousness of your spiritual Self, by dominating this body-idea with the spiritual consciousness that "I am not this psychophysical system, I am the ruler of the body, eternal, immortal, free; the essence of Spirit." You forget your divine heritage by identifying yourself with the body. But you can overcome this delusion and assert your real Self.

That is what Jesus Christ teaches us through His crucifixion: overcoming the body-idea by the spiritual conquest of the flesh; overcoming the lower self by the higher Self, the spiritual Self. That alone gives us immortality.

That is why we cannot understand the significance of resurrection without understanding the significance of the crucifixion. The cross is our symbol of that spiritual conquest.

The relationship between the cross and resurrection is most important, and has to be stressed. Jesus Christ said "Take up the cross and follow me." That is what He asks of us. It does not mean that each of you has to be crucified and become another Christ. But in order to reach the ideal He has set for us you have to follow Christ as far as you can, and make sincere efforts to walk in His footsteps.

The goal may be far away, but you can begin to move in that direction from wherever you are. Even a man who stands at the lowest foot of a mountain can look at the highest point, and gradually climb, step by step, until he reaches the top.

We have no excuse to say, "No, that teaching of non-resistance is obsolete these days. It cannot be practiced." Everything is practicable by efforts in the right direction in the right way. You just have to start.

By following in His footsteps you cannot be another Jesus Christ, but you can begin to follow His teaching from wherever you are.

You cannot follow Jesus Christ, or any great savior of the world, unless you believe in Him. Believing is much emphasized in the Christian church. But believing without following is of no importance — it is not enough.

> But be ye doers of the word, and not hearers only, deceiving your own selves.
>
> For if any be a hearer of the word, and not a doer, he is like a man beholding his natural face in a glass:
>
> For he beholdeth himself, and goeth his way, and straightway forgetteth what manner of man he was.
>
> (James 1:22-24)

If you do not make sincere efforts to follow His teaching according to your ability to do so, no matter how much you believe, you cannot be considered a follower of Jesus Christ. It is by taking up the cross daily and following Him that we can be as perfect, as divine, as free as He was. It is the cross that relates us to this resurrection of our own, to our own eternal life.

Through the fact of His crucifixion and resurrection Jesus Christ explained the mystery of death.

Death can take life out of the body, but it cannot affect the spiritual self of man. Man's real Self is a spiritual entity that leaves the body, yet is intact. Water can drown the body, but not the soul. Swords can pierce the body, but not the soul. Fire can burn the body, but not the soul. That is what Jesus Christ proves by His crucifixion and resurrection. Man is really Spirit, unborn, undying, unchanging.

Death is merely a change of condition.

As Sri Krishna says in the *Bhagavad Gita* (II:13): "Just as in this physical system there are changing states, babyhood, boyhood, youth, old age, so death is also a change of state." Death does not mean the extinction of personality or the annihilation of the person. It is just like changing one's clothing. You take off the present body and assume another.

It is true that death is very mysterious, but it is also inevitable. You cannot stay it even by ignoring it. All other facts are temporary and subject to change, but that you will grow older and die is a certain fact.

At the same time, death is so uncertain that you do not know when it will befall a person, or how, or where. It has no consideration for our deepest affection, for what we hold near and dear in our hearts. Death has no regard for the orphan's tears, the widow's wailings, or the lover's pangs of separation. Its icy touch extinguishes life forever and levels all.

Yet death is not as horrible as it appears to us. We can face death peacefully or painfully. It all depends on our attitude toward it. And our attitude toward life very much depends on our attitude toward death. We cannot know the meaning of life unless we know the meaning of death.

The great spiritual leaders tell us that there is nothing terrible about death. It is just a change of condition. You pass from one stage to another. Nothing is lost by death but this physical body.

All your excellences, and weaknesses, are stored in a

subtle body which is the repository of your powers, senses, and mind. If you acquire any special skills in this life, whether mental or physical, in athletics, art, music, mathematics, or anything else — any powers you acquire will remain with you beyond death. This is guaranteed by the law of *karma*.

When you leave an old house to move to a new one, you take all your furniture and possessions with you, leaving the empty house behind. Similarly, in death you actually take with you the powers of your organs and senses, your virtues and vices, your skills and all your faculties, leaving behind only the empty shell of the physical body.

So there is nothing to be afraid of in death. Whatever good you acquire will go with you; you will never lose it.

But remember that the Supreme Good is God. The more you turn your thoughts toward God, the greater will be your freedom in this life. And the more peacefully you will be able to face death.

If this human body were the whole of our existence, if it constituted the prime factor in our personality, then death would be the inevitable end of our existence. But there *is* something in the human personality which can exist apart from and independent of this physical body; so we will survive what we call death.

This body is not lasting and real. Regardless of what you do for it, wrinkles will appear in your face and your body will grow old and degenerate, if your life is not cut short. There is no method by which you can make this body eternal — it is only temporary. Death turns our minds away from our bodies, from the unreal to the Real, from the transitory to the Eternal.

In the *Katha Upanishad* there is a story of a Brahmin youth who was so daring that he wanted to know the secret of death. So he went to the abode of Yama, the king of death, to find out.

"Some people say that when a person dies he is completely annihilated," the youth said. "Others say that he continues to exist. What is the real truth about death? I want to know."

"Do not ask me this question," replied Yama. "This is very subtle. Neither the living nor the dead know it. Even the gods and angels do not know the secret of death. Ask me anything else and I will tell you. But this is my greatest secret."

Yama then offered the youth many temptations, both earthly and celestial, to test his sincerity in wanting to know this secret of all secrets. But the youth rejected them all, knowing them to be only transitory. So Yama relented and told the youth the way to the most priceless secret of all.

"The truth beyond death," Yama said, "does not become manifest to those who are dominated by worldly charms. Persons who do not care for the Eternal cannot know the secret of death. When you are quite ready to dedicate your life to the search for the Eternal, for the quest of the Supreme Being, only then can you know the secret of death. And unless you know that secret, again and again you will die and come under my subjection."

In this way death turns our minds from the superficial

to the deepest realities. Death says that you are not a permanent resident of this world; you are only a transient. All your relationships on earth — with your home, your possessions, your family and friends — all these are just temporary. From the temporal you should turn your thoughts to the Eternal. This is the message death brings us.

Dying just once does not end it all, because a person will be born again and again until he can work through his attachments in life. We cannot escape death by fearing it, or by taking refuge in temporal objects. You must seek God to know the secret of death.

Like Jesus Christ, we should have no fear in facing death. If you face death rightly, you will have no pain. You will be able to leave the body just as if you were shedding a coat.

However if you desperately cling to the transitory things you have to leave at the time of death, you will suffer great agony in dying. As long as you live in this world, you need money, friends, loved ones, joy of living, and a healthy body. But you must know that these things are not permanent, and they are not really yours.

You should not do everything for the sake of the body and forget the higher, lasting purpose of your life. St. Paul says in I Corinthians (6:19-20):

> Know ye not that your body is the temple of the Holy Ghost which is in you, which ye have of God, and ye are not your own?

> For ye are bought with a price: therefore glorify God in your body, and in your spirit, which are God's.

Live in the world, care for everything in this world, but do so for the sake of spiritual development, for the sake of the Supreme Lord. That is what is meant by overcoming the flesh. With this attitude you will die peacefully, free of the body and everything transitory, including death.

Jesus Christ has taught us through His crucifixion and resurrection the very secret of death, and the way to conquer it. By following His example, we must rise from the body-idea to the spiritual Consciousness, from the lower self to the Self of all.

For Jesus Christ, the same divine Spirit pervaded all beings. Established in that Consciousness, He practiced non-resistance and allowed Himself to be crucified, blessing those that crucified Him. As it is said in the *Upanishads:*

> He who knows his real Self as one with the universal Spirit, who sees his very Self enfolding all beings, whom can he hate?

> His heart accepts the whole universe as his own. He continually performs service to all beings. He can hate no one, and is equal to friend and foe alike.

Jesus Christ did not succumb to death because He realized Himself as one with God, ever beyond the body. The cross is our symbol of that crucifixion of the flesh. Death is only for the physical body, but the Spirit is everlasting.

CHAPTER XIV

Resurrection
and Everlasting Life

J ESUS Christ was crucified and buried on Good Friday, and arose from the dead to appear before Mary Magdalene and His disciples the following Sunday. Easter day is commemorative of that great occasion, the resurrection of Jesus Christ. The festival of Easter, however, did not originate with His resurrection.

Man's conception of resurrection is very old, and probably came from observing the cycles of nature. Originally Easter was a spring festival, universally observed at the time of the vernal equinox, which occurs about the twenty-first of March. The word Easter comes from *Eastre*, the name of the Anglo-Saxon goddess of dawn.

Common to all humanity, Easter celebrated the advent of spring in the world, when there is a resurgence of life after the death of winter. Trees and plants are dressed anew in green leaves; flowers put forth colorful blossoms; birds come out of their hiding places and sing beautiful songs. The sun shines soft and warm, and human hearts are filled with inspiration and vitality to see the many beauties of nature.

In almost all parts of the world, people spontaneously expressed this joyousness of feeling with days of festivity and thanks. The resurrection of Jesus Christ easily became associated with the resurrection of nature which brings joy to every human heart. Though the name Easter was retained, people forgot its secular significance, and its meaning is now wholly religious.

In the Bible we find belief in resurrection, or the renewal of life in the dead body, common among the Jewish people. They believed that all dead bodies would arise at doomsday, with the end of the world and the final judgment of the Lord. Those that had led virtuous lives would have eternal life in Heaven, while those who had led lives of sin and corruption would be doomed to eternal death and damnation. The word resurrection is not actually used in the Old Testament, but the idea is there.

> And many of them that sleep in the dust of the earth shall awake, some to everlasting life, and some to shame and everlasting contempt.   (Daniel 12:2)

The Jewish people also had a strong belief that the time would come when God would revive His Israel. In Isaiah's prayer to the Lord he says:

> Thy dead men shall live, together with my dead body shall they arise. Awake and sing, ye that dwell in dust: for thy dew is as the dew of herbs, and the earth shall cast out the dead.

> He shall cause them that come of Jacob to take root: Israel shall blossom and bud, and fill the face of the world with fruit.   (Isaiah 26:19; 27:6)

This re-establishment of Israel as a nation that Isaiah prayed for is also spoken of as a resurrection, and many hold that no more than this was meant by Isaiah. Still, we find that resurrection had two different significances in the minds of the Jewish people. One was this revival of the nation of Israel, and the second meaning was the rising of the dead at doomsday.

In the New Testament St. Paul has given another meaning to resurrection. In his first letter to the Corinthians we read:

> But some man will say, How are the dead raised up? and with what body do they come?
>
> Thou fool, that which thou sowest is not quickened, except it die:
>
> All flesh is not the same flesh: but there is one kind of flesh of man, another flesh of beasts, another of fishes, and another of birds.
>
> There are also celestial bodies, and bodies terrestrial: but the glory of the celestial is one, and the glory of the terrestrial is another.
>
> So also is the resurrection of the dead. It is sown in corruption, it is raised in incorruption: It is sown a natural body; it is raised a spiritual body. There is a natural body, and there is a spiritual body. (I Cor. 15:35,36,39,40,42,44)

It is evident from St. Paul's words he did not think that resurrection is actually this physical body rising from the dead. It is the spiritual body that rises. But spiritual body does not mean a body made of Spirit. Spirit cannot be changed in any way. It is too pure, too perfect to be molded into a physical being or any kind of form.

St. Paul meant a body made of such fine, subtle elements that spiritual consciousness could be manifest through it. That is the kind of spiritual body one gets in resurrection.

According to Vedanta also, it is possible that a person can retain that subtle body if he is worthy of resurrection. It is not the same as the gross physical body which succumbs to death. That subtle body is a physical body, but composed of extremely fine material elements, which not everyone can see.

When a great spiritual personality leaves the physical body he lives in the Consciousness of the Supreme Self, so much so that if he desires he can be completely absorbed or merged in the Supreme Spirit. But perhaps because of his love for humanity, he may not merge with God but retain his individuality. To do this, he has to retain the mind and an associated physical form.

Just as we depend on our bodies for perception, without a physical form the mind could not contact this physical universe. So he retains the physical form in which he lived while on earth, but it is not the same physical body of flesh and blood. It is a form made of very fine physical elements, almost an ethereal body, which is a fit vehicle for the expression of spiritual Consciousness.

The freedom, wisdom, love, and joy of a great spiritual leader are in no way restricted by that physical form. It is virtually a spiritual body, because it does not limit spiritual Consciousness in any way. When St. Paul says that "flesh and blood cannot inherit the kingdom of God" (I Cor. 15:50), he infers such a spiritual body.

For the great souls this body is merely a physical vehicle which they use to appear to whomever they choose. It is so fine, so pervasive, that it can even penetrate matter.

We find in the Gospel of St. John (20:19), that after His resurrection Jesus Christ entered a room where His disciples were gathered even though the doors remained closed. This happened again eight days later (20:26). If He wore the same physical body of flesh and blood that was crucified, Jesus Christ could never have appeared to His disciples in this manner.

Sri Ramakrishna also appeared to a select few after his death in the year 1886. He passed away just after one o'clock in the morning, and when the doctors had pronounced his body dead, it was cremated. That same evening he appeared to his virgin wife, the Holy Mother.

According to Hindu custom, widows give up all bodily decorations. They wear a plain white sari without borders, and remove all jewelry and ornaments. But as the Holy Mother was removing her bracelets, Sri Ramakrishna appeared to her and said, "What are you doing? I have not gone away. I have just passed from one room to another." Holy Mother understood that she need not live like a widow, since there was no death for Sri Ramakrishna.

From that time on she wore a sari with a thin red border, and kept two gold bracelets. On later occasions also, the Holy Mother and other disciples saw Sri Ramakrishna in a physical form as he used to be.

So resurrection, according to the Hindu view, is not the reviving of a particular body of flesh and blood. For the great spiritual personalities, another subtle physical body is formed and they contact their devotees through that body.[1] Resurrection and eternal life do not depend on the revival of a body, whether it is a subtle spiritual body or a gross physical body. Vedanta holds that the body is not an essential part of one's nature.

Our real nature is pure Spirit, undying, which can exist even without this body. Real life depends on the state of the mind, and not that of the body. As St. Paul said in his Epistle to the Romans (8:6): "For to be carnally minded is death; but to be spiritually minded is life and peace."

It is not just the body that makes you living or dead, it is your inner consciousness. If you are carnally minded, even though your body is alive, you are actually dead. As long as you identify yourself with this physical body, you are constantly subject to the round of birth, growth, decay, and death. You are already dead, from the highest spiritual standpoint. By being carnally minded, we create our own bondage and death.

The moment you overcome the delusion of the body-idea and know that you are unchanging Spirit, there is no death for you — you are resurrected. By being spiritually minded, you become aware of your unity with the Supreme

[1]Ghosts also appear in a body of very fine physical elements after death, but they appear in a certain place because of very strong attachments at the time of death. They have no control over their ghost body, and live in darkness after death just as they did when they were living on earth. Eventually they must be reborn on the human plane.

Being. That is life, truly speaking.

The great spiritual leaders like Jesus Christ and Sri Ramakrishna are our demonstrations of that principle of everlasting life. They lived with full spiritual Consciousness, never identifying themselves with the physical body. Their resurrections were for the good of others, for they were ever beyond death.

We are shown by their exemplary lives that it is not the body that creates our bondage and death. It is not the body in any form that leads us to freedom or immortality. Jesus Christ and Sri Ramakrishna prove that even while living in this body, one can gain real life by realizing the Spirit within.

Jesus Christ said "I am the resurrection, and the life: he that believeth in me, though he were dead, yet shall he live: And whosoever liveth and believeth in me shall never die." (St. John 11:25-26) By following the example and teachings of the great spiritual personalities, we too can attain resurrection and everlasting life.

Index

Allah, 53

Arjuna, 105-06

asceticism, 20-21

atman, 138*n,* 141-42

avatar, 32

baptism, 137, 143

belief, without following, 178

Bhagavad Gita, 11*n,* 25*n,* 41, 127
(II:13), 179; (IV:5,7,8), 35;
(IV:6), 37; (IV:9), 166; (VII:14),
25; (VIII:14,15), 146; (IX:11), 36;
(IX:22), 133; (IX:27), 160-61;
(IX:30,31), 131; (X:8), 25;
(XII:6,7), 133

Bhagavatam, 23*n,* 29-30, 99-100,
105

Bible, setting of, 68-69
  I. Cor. (3:16), 94; (6:19,20), 182;
    (10:31), 161; (15:35,36,39,40,
    42,44), 186; (15:50), 187-88
  Daniel (12:2), 185
  Ephesians (2:5), 26, 133
  Galatians (6:5,7-9), 144; (6:7), 22
  Isaiah (26:19; 27:6), 185
  James (1:22-24), 178
  Jude (21), 30
  Romans (6:14), 134; (8:6), 174,
    189
  St. John (1:1-4,14), 27; (1:14),
    33; (3:1-8), 136; (4:19-24), 148;
    (4:48), 59; (6:26,27), 60; (6:35),
    26; (8:12), 165; (8:32), 26; (8:31-
    36), 164; (8:42), 36; (9:2), 22;
    (10:17,18), 175; (10:37,38), 59;
    (11:25,26), 190; (12:37), 59;
    (20:19,26), 188
  St. Luke (1:30-31,34-35), 48;
    (8:10), 57; (9:27), 88; (9:28,29),
    51; (11:9), 130; (17:20,21), 88;
    (18:28-30), 24
  St. Mark (1:15), 83; (9:2,3), 51;
    (10:17,18), 125; (10:21), 57;
    (10:35-40), 87
  St. Matthew (1:20-21), 48; (3:2),
    83; (5:8), 170; (5:16,20,48), 86;
    (5:38-44), 97-98, 176; (6:19,20),
    86; (6:22), 27; (6:33), 26, 134;
    (10:37), 30; (10:39), 129; (13:31-
    33), 89; (17:1,2), 50; (17:11-13),
    21; (18:21,22), 161-62; (22:37,
    38), 30; (25:34), 85; (26:52),
    175

body: city of *Brahman,* 92; death
  of, 174, 178-79, 182; God in, 167-
  68; -idea, effect of, 139; -idea,
  overcoming, 143, 176-77, 183;
  karma and, 179-80; mistaken
  identity with, 16, 93, 137, 141;
  not the real self, 90, 141;
  resurrection of, 185-86, 189-90;
  Shankara's view of, 137-39*n,*
  141-42; subtle spiritual, 186-89

bondage: rescue from, 35, 44, 46,
  60; way out of, 27, 40, 165-66,
  169, 172; we create, 126-27, 189-
  90

Brahman, 28*n,* 92, 94

Brahmanas, 28

Buddha, 32, 35, 39; and non-
  resistance, 23, 99

Buddhism, 18, 19, 20, 23, 25

Christianity: devotion in, 25, 30-31, 44-45; distinctive elements, 18, 20-21; Incarnation, 28-29, 30-35, 43; grace in, 25-26; influences, 18-21, 28; Sri Ramakrishna and, 53-54

cognition, 139-41, 152

Confucius, 33, 98

consciousness: God-, 85, 88-89; inner, 172; principle of, 140-41, 152; spiritual, 143, 145-46, 176, 183; Supreme, 90-93, 151-53

creation, 27-29, 33-34

cross, 82, 176-78, 183

crucifixion, 174-78, 183

death, 174, 178-79, 180, 185-87; by being carnally minded, 174, 189; and *karma,* 116, 119; Jesus Christ, 174, 183; message of, 180-82; Sri Ramakrishna, 188; overcoming, 189-90

desires, sense, 139

devotion: as basic attitude, 160; in Christianity, 25, 30-31, 44-45; in Hinduism, 25, 29-31, 44-45, 133; to God, 25, 166-68; to God's Incarnation, 44

dharma, 10-11, 17

discipline, spiritual, 50, 53, 61, 89

dualities: and the Word, 33; disillusioned with, 13, 106, 125, 145; going beyond, 124-25, 144, 145; inevitable, 13-14, 17, 124, 144

Easter, 184

ego: apparent self, 140; giving up, 127-29, 131; limitations of, 125-26, 130, 135

Elias, 21

Essenes, 20-21

eternal, everlasting life, 24, 30, 185; attaining, 77, 174, 189-90; longing for, 125, 145

ethical life, highest level, 103

ethical principle, 57, 101, 107-08

evil: deeds, 81, 135; good and, 13, 124, 131; returning good for, 23, 98-99, 105; tendencies, 115

faith, self-deception in, 158-60

forgiveness, 102-03

freedom: of choice and action, 111, 117-19; desire for, 124-25, 145; from sin, 165; gaining, 41, 46, 169-70, 172-73, 176, 180; Incarnation and, 166; real, complete, 125-26, 169, 172; sacrificing, 129

goal, Supreme, 14-17, 39, 62, 106-07

good: absolute, 13, 125-26, 180; deeds and actions, 121, 123-24, 135; and evil, 13, 124, 131-32; returning for evil, 23, 98-99, 105; forces, 90

Gospels, *see* Bible

grace, 123-135; and divine law, 110; attaining, 46, 122, 127-30, 135; fulfills material needs, 133-34; in Hinduism and Christianity, 25-26, 133-34; in human form, 33; of Buddha, Jesus Christ, and Sri Ramakrishna, 132-33; proof of, 43-44; too tender for defiance, 130; works in two ways, 134

Greece: as voice of Europe, 69; in sixth cent. B.C., 99*n;* religion, 20

hatred, harmful effects of, 102

heart: abode of *Brahman,* 92, 94; cry within, 14; encouraging message to, 88; filled with devotion, 44; God within, 90, 94-95, 155-56; in touch with the divine, 81; pure in, 26, 170; seeking God, 45, 172; Spirit consciousness within, 92, 152; temple in, 155

Hillel, Rabbi, 98

Hinduism: belief in Incarnation, 28-29, 30-35, 43; definition of, 9-10; devotion in, 25, 29-31, 44-45; foreign designation, 9-10; grace in, 25, 133; influence on Christianity, 18-20; non-resistance in, 23-24; spiritual disciplines, 53; view of Incarnation, 28-31, 33-35; view of spiritual teachers, 38

ignorance: cause of suffering, 165, 169; freedom from, 165, 173; God and Spirit hidden by, 27, 77; veil of, 16

immortality, 24, *see also* eternal life

Incarnation: appearance of, 36, 39, 43; as proof of divine love, 44-45, 167; best conception of God, 45, 65-66; beyond bondage, 36; Hindu and Christian views of, 28-31, 33-35, 43; definition, 32; freedom through, 165-68; from the Word-*Vak,* 28-29, 33-34; Jesus Christ and Sri Ramakrishna, 52, 54-55; mission of, 32, 43, 46, 58; proof of, 36-37

India: foreign designation, 9-10; renunciation in, 24-25

Ishamasi (Jesus Christ, q.v.), 53

Islam, 18; Sri Ramakrishna turned to, 53

Jesus Christ: belief in, 165, 178; as the best of His race, 68; birth, 47-49; relation to body, 72; crucifixion, 174-78, 183; did not assert Himself as good, 125-26; embodiment of Spirit, 73, 183; ethical precepts of, 57; as the exemplar of His teachings, 40, 175-76; on forgiveness, 102-03; grace of, 132; as Incarnation, 28, 32, 34, 39, 165; influences on, 21; miracles, 59-60; mission of, 58, 60; non-resistance, 23, 40, 97-98, 175-76, 183; overcame the flesh, 177; parables, 57; power, 60; practical nature of, 71; and Sri Ramakrishna, 47-62; Sri Ramakrishna's vision of, 53-54; reincarnation familiar to, 21-22; on renunciation, 24, 77-78; resurrection, 177-78, 184-85, 190; spiritual discipline, 50; in subtle body, 188; teachings of, 55-56; teachings, in stages, 76; transfiguration, 50-51; unselfish, 78-79; use of *Kingdom of God,* 83-89; Swami Vivekananda on, 63-82

John the Baptist, 20-21

John, St., and the Word, 28

Judaism, 20, 67

karma, 110-122; in death, 116, 119;

defined, 22-23, 111-12; and ego-idea, 122, 126-28; explains inequalities, 22, 117; inevitable, 118-19; results of, 112-116, 126; St. Paul refers to, 22; works in two ways, 119-20; *-yoga,* 127, 135, 145

kingdom of God — kingdom of heaven, 83-96; attaining, 39, 147; celestial dominion, 86; earthly, 84-85; as God-consciousness, 88-89; Jewish conception, 83-84; in parables, 89; used three ways, 85; within you, 27, 88, 90, 96

Krishna, Sri, 23n; devotion and grace, 25, 29-30, 133; Incarnation, 32, 35, 39, 166; non-attachment, 40; non-resistance, 23, 99-100, 105-106

Lao-tse, 33; good for evil, 98

love: demonstration of, 45; God's, 43-46, 166; for God, 25, 30, 44-45, 162, 166-68; Jesus Christ, 175-76; non-resistance, 98-99, 106

Mahabharata, 11-12

material: life, needs moral basis, 40; possessions, God gives, 133

meditation, 153, 154, 155, 167-68, 172; Jesus Christ, 50; *samadhi* from, 51; Sri Ramakrishna, 53

mercy, 110, 122, 131-32, 153, *see also* grace

mind: condition of, 90; not the real person, 93-94; real Self beyond, 91; soundness of, 12; Spirit works through, 92

mind, purification of, 14-15; how to attain, 95-105; needed to perceive truth, 26, 137, 170-71; results of, 13, 26-27, 105, 126, 143; is the search for God, 27

minded, carnally-spiritually, 174, 189

miracles, greatest, 42, 61; of Jesus Christ, 59-60; of Sri Ramakrishna, 60-61

Misra, 54-55n

moral: decline, 42; principles, observance of, 12-13, 95-96, 143-45; results of *karma,* 114-15

morality, essentially spirituality, 100

Moses, 33, 38-39

New Testament, validity of, 74; *see also* Bible

non-attachment, 44

non-resistance, 23-24, 97-109; Jesus Christ as example of, 40, 175-76, 183

organs: objects of cognition, 139-41; Spirit shines through, 92-93

Orient, setting of Bible, 68-69

Origen, 22

parables and stories, 57-58; holy man and the scorpion, 107-08; kite and the crows, 58; leaven and mustard seed, 89; parable of the saw, 99; pundit and the milkmaid, 158-59; student and the piece of cake, 137-38; thief and treasure, 157; youth and the king of death, 181

perfection: of existence, 15, 91; of

God, 45, 125; reaching, 146, 173; search for, 15, 125

Philo, 19; and the Word, 28

Plato, 19*n*, 23

prayer: Jesus Christ, 51, 55; results of, 51, 145; Sri Ramakrishna, 53, 55; when you can't meditate, 155

purification: inner, 145, 172; *see also* mind

purity, necessary to know Spirit, 76-77; through *karma yoga*, 128, 145;

Pythagoras, 19

rajas, 103-05

Ramakrishna, Sri, 17*n*, 37*n*, 190; appearance after death, 188; approaches to God, 53, 61-62; birth, 47-49; on freedom, 118; grace of, 132-33; on great teachers, 38; Incarnation, 37*n*, 167; and Jesus Christ, 47-62; vision of Jesus Christ, 53-54; miracles, 60-61; with Misra, 54-55*n;* parable of kite and crows, 58; *samadhi*, 51-52; spiritual disciplines, 50, 53, 61; story of pundit and milkmaid, 158; teachings, 55; toward other religions, 150

reality, Supreme, 92, 94

rebirth: physical, 142, 146, 182; spiritual, 137, 143-44, 146-47

reincarnation, 21-22, 23, 142, 146

religion, as basic attitude, 160-61; basic truth of, 17; when it declines, 42; different stages, 74-75; human, 66; necessity of

mankind, 17; pathway to God, 17, 53, 55; practical, 71; private affair, 160; respect for, 55

renunciation: in India, 24-25; taught by Jesus Christ, 24, 77-78

resurrection: attaining, 189-90; of the dead, 185; of Israel, 186; of Jesus Christ, 177-78, 184-85, 190

salvation: condition for, 76, 78; through spiritual teachers, 38-39

samadhi, 51-52

sattva, 103-05

saviors, 38-40, 46, 58

secular life: limitations, 10, 14; leads to spiritual, 11-13

self: -awareness, 91; of all, 15, 173, 183; inmost, 91, 96, 100; of man, 27; physical, 139; real, 15, 91, 101, 142, 145, 151, 174, 177-78; -resignation, 129; spiritual, 92, 152, 168-69, 176-77; Supreme, 27, 95, 100, 154; -surrender, 25, 127-18, 131, 134; -understanding, 153-54

selfishness, 100-02

Shankara, 28, 138*n;* view of body, 137-39, 141-42; view of human birth, 139*n*

sin: freedom from, 134, 165; -ful persons, 132

sincerity, in worship, 156-58, 160

soul, 75; to reach, 92

Spirit: being born of, 137, 146; consciousness, 146, 183; within the heart, 94, 108; Incarnation, 36; Jesus Christ was, 73; knowing, 76-77, 189-90, 153-54; man is, 15-16, 91, 96, 116, 178; unlike matter, 151, 168; shines within all, 92-93, 152-53; worship in, 148-156

spiritual: Consciousness, 143, 145-46, 176, 183; discipline, 50, 53, 61, 89; self, 92, 152, 168-69, 176-77

stories, *see* parables

Supreme Being, 14, 15-16, 17, 128, 146; pathways to, 17, 53; Word and, 33

tamas, 103-04

transfiguration, of Jesus Christ, 50-51

transformation, through great saviors, 40-41, 45, 60-61

truth: about death, 181; about Jesus Christ, 165-66; in forgiveness, 103; is God, 79; imitation of, 74; about Incarnation, 166-69; about Kingdom of God, 88-89; never from error to, 75; of religious life, 162; perception of, 26; Sri Ramakrishna, 53; shall make you free, 26, 164-65, 169-70, 173; Supreme, 169-73; worship in, 156-163

Uddhava, 29-30, 105-06

Upanishads, 24, 146, 156; *Katha,* 95, 181; *Kena,* 94

unselfishness, 78, 101

Vak, 28-29

values, secular and absolute, 40

Vedanta: body, 92; defined, 9-10; good, 13; kingdom of God, 96; man's real nature, 79-80; mental health, 12; different religions, 17; search for God, 15-16; Supreme Being, 15-16; virtue, 11, 144

Vedas, 9-10

virtue: basis of life, 12; in non-resistance, 98; path of, 11, 95, 105, 143-44, 169

Vivekachudamani, 138n, 139, 141, 142

Vivekananda, Swami, 17; on Christ, 63-82; on thinking of God, 45; on non-resistance, 106

Word, the, 27-29, 33-35

worship: of Jesus Christ, 74; methods, 150-51; 154-55; mistakes in, 150; with sincerity, 156-58, 160; in spirit, 148-156; in truth, 156-163

Yama, king of death, 181

yoga, karma, 127, 135, 145